Reading and Note Taking Study Guide

UNITED STATES
HISTORY
RECONSTRUCTION TO THE PRESENT

PEARSON

Boston, Massachusetts • Chandler, Arizona • Glenview, Illinois • New York, New York

Acknowledgments

Grateful acknowledgment is made to the following for copyrighted material:

Images:
Cover: Robert Harding Picture Library/Alamy

PEARSON

ISBN-13: 978-0-32-888035-5

ISBN-10:   0-32-888035-3

7 19

Contents

United States History Reconstruction to the Present
Reading and Note Taking Study Guide

How to use the *Reading and Note Taking Study Guide*

The **Reading and Note Taking Study Guide** will help you better understand the content of Pearson *United States History Reconstruction to the Present*. This section will also develop your reading, vocabulary, and note taking skills. Each study guide consists of three components. The first component focuses on developing graphic organizers that will help you take notes as you read.

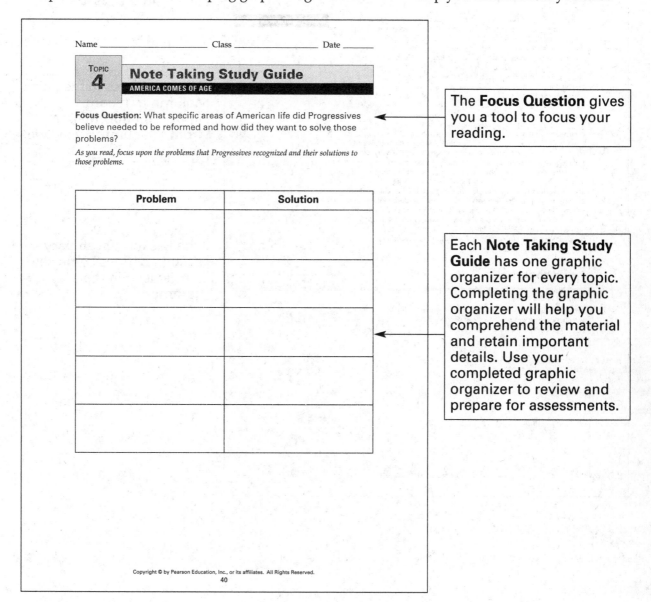

Name _____ Class _____ Date _____

TOPIC 4 — Note Taking Study Guide
AMERICA COMES OF AGE

Focus Question: What specific areas of American life did Progressives believe needed to be reformed and how did they want to solve those problems?

As you read, focus upon the problems that Progressives recognized and their solutions to those problems.

Problem	Solution

40

The **Focus Question** gives you a tool to focus your reading.

Each **Note Taking Study Guide** has one graphic organizer for every topic. Completing the graphic organizer will help you comprehend the material and retain important details. Use your completed graphic organizer to review and prepare for assessments.

The second component highlights the central themes, issues, and concepts of each lesson.

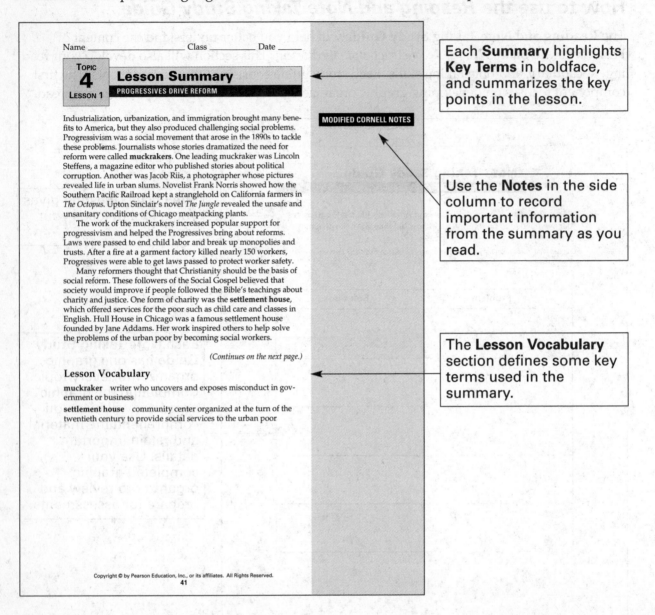

Name _____ Class _____ Date _____

TOPIC 4
LESSON 1
Lesson Summary
PROGRESSIVES DRIVE REFORM

Each **Summary** highlights **Key Terms** in boldface, and summarizes the key points in the lesson.

MODIFIED CORNELL NOTES

Industrialization, urbanization, and immigration brought many benefits to America, but they also produced challenging social problems. Progressivism was a social movement that arose in the 1890s to tackle these problems. Journalists whose stories dramatized the need for reform were called **muckrakers**. One leading muckraker was Lincoln Steffens, a magazine editor who published stories about political corruption. Another was Jacob Riis, a photographer whose pictures revealed life in urban slums. Novelist Frank Norris showed how the Southern Pacific Railroad kept a stranglehold on California farmers in *The Octopus*. Upton Sinclair's novel *The Jungle* revealed the unsafe and unsanitary conditions of Chicago meatpacking plants.

The work of the muckrakers increased popular support for progressivism and helped the Progressives bring about reforms. Laws were passed to end child labor and break up monopolies and trusts. After a fire at a garment factory killed nearly 150 workers, Progressives were able to get laws passed to protect worker safety.

Many reformers thought that Christianity should be the basis of social reform. These followers of the Social Gospel believed that society would improve if people followed the Bible's teachings about charity and justice. One form of charity was the **settlement house**, which offered services for the poor such as child care and classes in English. Hull House in Chicago was a famous settlement house founded by Jane Addams. Her work inspired others to help solve the problems of the urban poor by becoming social workers.

(Continues on the next page.)

Lesson Vocabulary

muckraker   writer who uncovers and exposes misconduct in government or business

settlement house   community center organized at the turn of the twentieth century to provide social services to the urban poor

Use the **Notes** in the side column to record important information from the summary as you read.

The **Lesson Vocabulary** section defines some key terms used in the summary.

41

The third component consists of review questions that assess your understanding of the lesson.

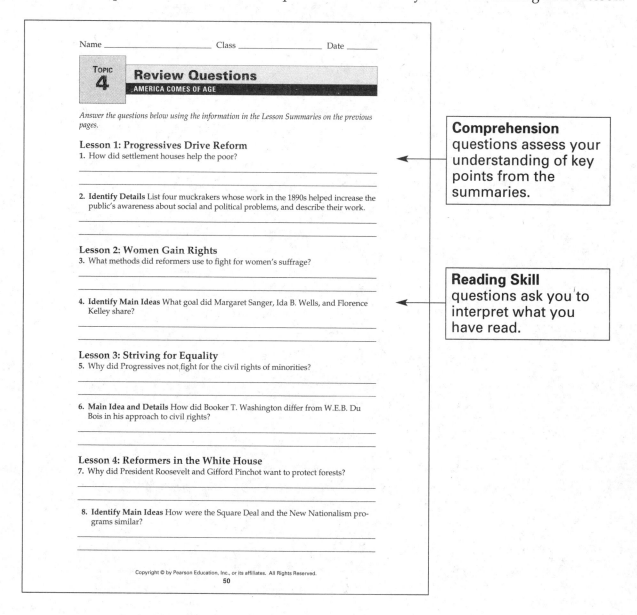

Name _____ Class _____ Date _____

Review Questions
AMERICA COMES OF AGE

Answer the questions below using the information in the Lesson Summaries on the previous pages.

Lesson 1: Progressives Drive Reform
1. How did settlement houses help the poor?
_____
_____

2. **Identify Details** List four muckrakers whose work in the 1890s helped increase the public's awareness about social and political problems, and describe their work.
_____
_____

Lesson 2: Women Gain Rights
3. What methods did reformers use to fight for women's suffrage?
_____
_____

4. **Identify Main Ideas** What goal did Margaret Sanger, Ida B. Wells, and Florence Kelley share?
_____
_____

Lesson 3: Striving for Equality
5. Why did Progressives not fight for the civil rights of minorities?
_____
_____

6. **Main Idea and Details** How did Booker T. Washington differ from W.E.B. Du Bois in his approach to civil rights?
_____
_____

Lesson 4: Reformers in the White House
7. Why did President Roosevelt and Gifford Pinchot want to protect forests?
_____
_____

8. **Identify Main Ideas** How were the Square Deal and the New Nationalism programs similar?
_____
_____

Comprehension questions assess your understanding of key points from the summaries.

Reading Skill questions ask you to interpret what you have read.

Name _____ Class _____ Date _____

Focus Question: How did the Civil War shape America?

As you read, note the causes of the Civil War and the effects the Civil War had on the country.

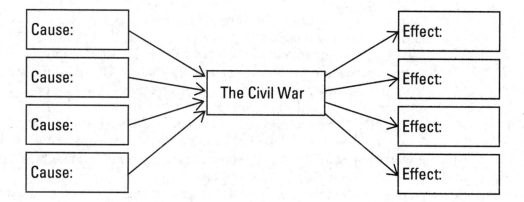

Lesson Summary

COLONIES AND REVOLUTION

MODIFIED CORNELL NOTES

Spain established colonies in the present-day Southwest and Florida, where forts called **presidios** were set up for protection and missions were set up to convert Native Americans to Christianity. The French established **colonies** in Canada and along the Mississippi River valley in Louisiana.

In 1607, the English established their first enduring settlement at Jamestown in Virginia. The Virginia colonists elected a legislature known as the House of Burgesses. To the north, the English established a cluster of colonies called New England. Most of the colonists there were devout Protestants called "Puritans." The first English to land in Plymouth adopted the Mayflower Compact, which provided a framework for **self-government**.

The English developed other colonies between New England and Virginia. The English colonists brought ideas about democracy and government with them to America. During the 1700s, ideas based on the Enlightenment, a philosophy that taught that human reason could solve all problems, circulated among well-educated colonists. Frenchman Baron de Montesquieu and Englishman John Locke were two thinkers who applied reason to government and politics.

In the 1740s, concern about more rational religious services and decreasing church attendance led to a religious movement called the Great Awakening. The rise of new organized churches resulting from this movement increased **tolerance** of religious differences. Many colonists also came to believe that if they could decide how to worship God, they could also decide how to govern themselves.

Between 1689 and 1763, the British and French fought a series of costly wars. The British Parliament wanted the colonists to pay new taxes to help the empire. The colonists resisted the taxes, asserting their rights as Englishmen. They cited the Magna Carta (1215), which limited the power of the king, and also the English Bill of Rights (1689), which was a written list of freedoms and which blocked the king from levying taxes without the permission of Parliament. The colonists would pay taxes levied only by their own elected **assemblies**.

(Continues on the next page.)

Lesson Vocabulary

presidio a military fort

colony a region that is controlled by a country, often a far-away country

self-government a system of government in which the people of an area control their own government and are not ruled or governed by an outside authority

tolerance the willingness to respect the beliefs of others

assembly a group of people gathered for a common purpose, often to make rules and laws

REVIEW TOPIC

LESSON 1

Lesson Summary
COLONIES AND REVOLUTION (continued)

War broke out between the colonies and the British in 1775, at Concord, Massachusetts. In 1776, the 13 colonies adopted the Declaration of Independence, drafted by Thomas Jefferson of Virginia, who was greatly influenced by the Enlightenment idea of people's natural rights. The first person to sign the Declaration was John Hancock, a wealthy merchant and leader of the Patriots in Massachusetts. The war continued until 1783, when the American colonists under the command of George Washington finally defeated the British army.

REVIEW TOPIC
LESSON 2
Lesson Summary
FOUNDING A NEW NATION

After winning their independence from Britain, the former American colonies became states. Each state created a constitution that established a **republican government**, or a government in which officials are representatives elected by the people. Most of these state constitutions included a **bill of rights**, a list of freedoms guaranteed by the state government.

In 1777, the 13 states adopted their first national constitution, the Articles of Confederation. The Articles gave Congress authority over the Northwest Territory, a vast area north of the Ohio River that stretched from Pennsylvania to the Mississippi River. In 1785 and 1787, Congress passed laws to manage this land.

Under the Articles, most power remained with the states. Without the ability to levy taxes, the federal government could not pay its immense war debt. Similarly, the weak confederation, or alliance of governments pledged to work together, could not defend American interests on the frontier.

Domestic troubles also began plaguing the young republic, including an economic depression and Shays' Rebellion, an armed uprising of Massachusetts farmers that was intended to shut down the courts and block foreclosures of farms. The rebellion highlighted the weaknesses of the national government.

In May 1787, the states sent delegates to a convention to amend the Articles of Confederation. The small states wanted to keep a loose confederation of states. In contrast, James Madison of Virginia advocated a national union that was both strong and republican.

The Great Compromise settled the differences between the two plans. In a concession to the smaller states, the Senate would equally represent every state by allowing just two senators per state. By contrast, in the House of Representatives granted more power to larger states because representation was based on population.

(Continues on the next page.)

Lesson Vocabulary

republican government   a government in which officials are representatives elected by the people; also known as a representative democracy

bill of rights   the protections for personal liberty that limit the power of the government over individuals

REVIEW TOPIC LESSON 2	**Lesson Summary**
	FOUNDING A NEW NATION (continued)

Southern delegates feared domination by the northern states, which had a larger white population. The delegates adopted the three-fifths clause. It counted each enslaved person as three fifths of a person, to be added to a state's free population, which boosted the number of the South's seats in the House of Representatives.

Before the new Constitution would go into effect, 9 of the 13 states had to **ratify**, or officially approve, it. Supporters of the Constitution, known as Federalists, wrote a series of letters to newspapers. These letters, collectively called *The Federalist Papers*, explained why they believed the nation needed a stronger federal government and how the new system of government would work.

Opponents, known as Antifederalists, objected to the Constitution because they thought it gave the national government far too much power. Because the most powerful argument of the Antifederalists was that the proposed Constitution lacked a bill of rights, the Federalists promised to add a bill of rights. In 1789, Congress approved 10 constitutional amendments that became the federal Bill of Rights.

The Constitution divided power between the states and the nation, which is known as **federalism**. The Constitution also promoted a **separation of powers** within the federal government by defining distinct executive, legislative, and judicial branches. Each branch had **checks and balances** on the others to prevent one branch from taking control of the government. The Constitution created a **limited government**, that is, the powers of government are specifically defined. At the same time, the founders worded parts of the Constitution to permit fexibility. Since its ratification, the Constitution has been amended 27 times.

Lesson Vocabulary

ratify   to officially approve

federalism   a system of government in which power is divided between a central government and member states

separation of powers   the distribution of power among the three branches of a government—executive, legislative, and judicial

checks and balances   a system that allows different branches of a government to override, or check and balance, the decisions of the other branches of the government in order to prevent abuse of power

limited government   a government that is limited in power by law, often through a written set of laws or constitution

REVIEW
TOPIC

LESSON 3

Lesson Summary

AMERICA IN THE EARLY 1800s

MODIFIED CORNELL NOTES

After the Revolutionary War, Secretary of the Treasury Alexander Hamilton created a financial plan to pay off the war debt. Hamilton's proposals were embraced by the newly formed Federalist Party but opposed by leaders such as Thomas Jefferson and James Madison, who wanted a limited government and an agrarian society. Critics from the South said that it favored merchants from the Northeast by compensating them with tax dollars. Jefferson and Madison and their mostly southern supporters formed the Democratic Republican Party to oppose Hamilton's agenda.

Thomas Jefferson was elected President in 1800. In 1803, Chief Justice John Marshall used the case of *Marbury* v. *Madison* to assert that the Supreme Court had the power of **judicial review**, that is, the power for courts to decide the constitutionality of law. Also in 1803, Jefferson bought a vast territory extending from the Mississippi River to the Rocky Mountains from France in the Louisiana Purchase.

In the early 1800s, the British navy had been seizing American sailors and merchant ships. Jefferson asked Congress to declare an **embargo** that stopped trade with Britain. The War of 1812 between Britain and the United States led to the end of tension with Britain. The United States won the war in 1815.

In 1817, President James Monroe issued the Monroe Doctrine. It declared that European monarchies had no business meddling with American republics. In return, the United States promised to stay out of European affairs.

The rise of war hero General Andrew Jackson in the 1820s shifted the politics of the nation. While the age of Jacksonian democracy expanded the concept of democracy, some policies of the Jackson era resulted in long-term political strife.

As President, Jackson urged Congress to pass the Indian Removal Act of 1830. This law sought to negotiate the peaceful exchange of Indian lands in the South for new lands in Indian Territory. Most Choctaws and Chickasaws agreed to accept lands in the West, but other groups resisted. In 1838, federal troops compelled more than 15,000 Cherokees to walk from the Southeast to Oklahoma along what came to be called the Trail of Tears.

(Continues on the next page.)

Lesson Vocabulary

judicial review   the power for courts to decide the constitutionality of law

embargo   a restriction on all trade with another country

Lesson Summary

AMERICA IN THE EARLY 1800s (continued)

Southerners benefited from Indian removal, but they opposed the federal government's adoption of **protective tariffs**. South Carolina, relying on the doctrine of **nullification**, claimed that it could void, or nullify, unconstitutional laws within its borders. Jackson threatened to use troops to enforce federal law in South Carolina. At the same time, Congress reduced the tariff and the crisis passed.

In 1832, Congress voted to renew the charter for the second Bank of the United States, but Jackson vetoed the renewal. Supporters of the Bank formed the Whig Party in 1832. However, Jackson won re-election and took steps to finish off the Bank. Freed from federal regulation, state and private banks flooded the nation with paper money of uncertain value. Jackson's decision to stop accepting paper money for the purchase of federal land eventually let to the Panic of 1837, the nation's worst economic depression to that date.

Beginning in 1831, French aristocrat Alexis de Tocqueville undertook a study of American society and politics. He believed there were five important factors to the success of democracy in the United States: liberty, **egalitarianism**, individualism, **populism**, and **laissez-faire**.

In the United States, the Industrial Revolution took hold first in the Northeast, which had more water power than any other region. The invention of the cotton gin in 1793 made cotton the South's leading crop. While the Northeast industrialized, the southern states became more reliant on an agricultural economy fueled by slave labor.

Many people in the North were **abolitionists** who worked for the end of slavery. One influential abolitionist was Frederick Douglass, who was a former slave and a powerful speaker. Other abolitionists and free blacks organized a network known as the underground railroad to help slaves escape from the South to destinations in the North or in Canada.

(Continues on the next page.)

Lesson Vocabulary

protective tariffs   the taxes on imported goods designed to protect domestic industry

nullification   the idea that states could nullify, or void, any federal law they deemed unconstitutional

egalitarianism   the view that people are equal and should be treated the same

populism   the widespread participation of regular citizens in the political process and the inclusion of their concerns in political debates

laissez-faire   the absence of government control over personal and economic life

abolitionists   reformers who advocated a complete end to slavery

Lesson Summary

AMERICA IN THE EARLY 1800s (continued)

Abolitionism was part of a drive to reform American society in the early 1800s. This reform movement was partly created by the Second Great Awakening, a revival of religious feeling that led to an increase in participation in evangelical Protestant movements.

The emerging reform movements welcomed women. In 1848, Lucretia Mott and Elizabeth Cady Stanton, two prominent abolitionists, helped organize the Seneca Falls Convention. This meeting, the first of the **women's rights movement** in the United States, attracted hundreds of men and women. The delegates to the convention adopted a Declaration of Sentiments, declaring men and women to be equal. The convention inspired a generation of women's rights leaders, including Susan B. Anthony. However, the important goal of **suffrage**, or the right to vote, was not achieved until 1920.

By 1830, the United States had grown beyond its original territory, but American **expansionists** believed in Manifest Destiny, that is, the right of the nation to extend its territory across the continent to the Pacific Coast.

Americans had also begun to settle in Texas in the 1820s. In 1835, Texans rebelled against the Mexican government. In response, Mexican forces attacked the Texans. Led by Sam Houston, Texan forces crushed the Mexican army at the Battle of San Jacinto, forcing the Mexican general to sign a treaty recognizing Texan independence. The Mexican government refused to honor the terms of the treaty, and a border war persisted between Texas and Mexico.

President James K. Polk, an expansionist, endorsed the Texan and sent troops to occupy the contested territory. When a Mexican patrol clashed with U.S. soldiers, Congress declared war on Mexico.

In this one-sided war, the United States won every major battle. The defeated Mexicans made peace in the Treaty of Guadalupe Hidalgo. This treaty gave the United States possession of New Mexico and California and secured the Rio Grande as the southern boundary of Texas. The growing conflict between the northern and southern states was fueled by the debate over whether these new territories should be admitted as free or slave states.

Lesson Vocabulary

women's rights movement the campaign for equal rights for women

suffrage the right to vote

expansionists people who favor territorial growth

Lesson Summary

THE UNION IN CRISIS

MODIFIED CORNELL NOTES

During the Mexican-American War, the question of slavery in the West emerged as a major issue. In 1846, the Wilmot Proviso was introduced in Congress to ban slavery in any territory that the United States gained from Mexico as a result of the war. Although it never became law, it contributed to increasing tension over slavery.

In 1848, northern opponents of slavery formed the Free-Soil Party to prevent the expansion of slavery into the western territories. When California applied to enter the Union as a free state, Congress passed the Compromise of 1850, which allowed voters in the territories acquired from Mexico to decide the slavery issue for themselves. This approach was known as **popular sovereignty**.

The Compromise of 1850 also included a Fugitive Slave Act that required all citizens to help capture runaway slaves. Many Northerners resisted the law, and resentment against the act spurred Harriet Beecher Stowe to write the novel *Uncle Tom's Cabin*, a powerful condemnation of slavery. Opposition to slavery led to the creation of the new Republican Party in 1854.

In the same year, Congress passed the Kansas-Nebraska Act, which divided the Nebraska Territory into two territories. Voters in each territory would decide the issue of slavery. Soon, both proslavery and antislavery settlers were flocking to Kansas. Throughout the fall of 1856, there was so much violence perpetrated by both sides that the territory became known as "Bleeding Kansas." In 1861, Kansas finally entered the Union as a free state.

In the 1857 Supreme Court case *Dred Scott* v. *Sandford*, Chief Justice Roger Taney stated that African Americans were not citizens and, therefore, not entitled to sue in the courts. The Court also ruled that Congress did not have the power to ban slavery in any territory.

In the fall of 1859, radical abolitionist John Brown and a small band of followers seized the federal arsenal at Harpers Ferry, Virginia, hoping to inspire a slave uprising. Instead, Brown was caught and executed. The incident increased northern sympathy toward abolition but inflamed southern anger and suspicion.

In 1860, anxiety ran high in both the North and the South as the presidential election approached. During the election, the Democrats split into two parties. Northern Democrats backed Stephen A. Douglas, who supported popular sovereignty, while southern Democrats nominated Vice President John C. Breckinridge, who wanted to expand slavery into the territories.

(Continues on the next page.)

Lesson Vocabulary

popular sovereignty   a doctrine allowing new states to decide the issue of slavery for themselves

Lesson Summary

THE UNION IN CRISIS (continued)

MODIFIED CORNELL NOTES

The Republicans nominated Abraham Lincoln. Their platform called for an end to slavery in the territories. They stipulated that there should be no interference with slavery in the states where it already existed. The split in the Democratic Party kept those candidates from getting enough votes to win the election. Instead, Lincoln won even though he did not receive a single southern **electoral vote**.

When Lincoln's election was confirmed, South Carolina seceded from the Union. In the next few weeks, six other states of the Deep South seceded. In February 1861, they established the Confederate States of America. The Confederate constitution stressed each state's independence and protected slavery. The Confederacy chose former Mississippi senator Jefferson Davis as its President.

In an attempt to compromise with the South, Kentucky Senator John Crittenden proposed a new **constitutional amendment**. If it had passed, the Crittenden Compromise would have allowed slavery in western territories south of the Missouri Compromise line. In his last weeks in office, President Buchanan told Congress that he had no authority to prevent secession. A secret peace convention held in Washington also failed to reach a compromise that could save the Union.

Lesson Vocabulary

electoral vote   a vote cast by a member of the electoral college, the group of people who determine the winner of a presidential election

constitutional amendment   a change or modification to the Constitution

Lesson Summary
THE CIVIL WAR

Abraham Lincoln took office as the new President amid the turmoil of southern states seceding from the Union. In his inaugural address, Lincoln said that he did not intend to interfere with slavery in states where it existed. He intended to preserve the Union, but he would not start a war. When South Carolinians fired on Fort Sumter, a Union fort guarding the harbor at Charleston, President Lincoln called for 75,000 volunteers to fight against the Confederacy.

Between 1861 and 1865, the Union and the Confederacy fought each other in the Civil War. The urbanized North was able to produce the supplies necessary to wage war. Given such advantages, northerners anticipated a quick victory. By contrast, the more rural South had skillful and experienced military leaders, such as General Robert E. Lee.

The North adopted a strategy known as the Anaconda Plan, which aimed to starve the South into submission. The Confederacy, by contrast, simply had to survive until northerners became tired of fighting. Although each side won some battles, a stalemate developed. The combination of new weapons and limited medical care led to a high number of casualties.

In 1863, Lincoln issued the Emancipation Proclamation, which freed all slaves in areas rebelling against the Union. Although it did not immediately free any slaves, it redefined the war as being "about slavery."

Some northerners opposed Lincoln's conduct of the war. To deal with dissent, Lincoln suspended the constitutional right of **habeas corpus**, which guarantees that no one can be held in prison without specific charges being filed. As the war dragged on, the Union army experienced a shortage of volunteers. When Congress passed a **draft law** in 1863, requiring all able-bodied men between the ages of 20 and 45 to serve in the military if called, riots broke out in several northern cities. Meanwhile, the South was struggling with economic problems. Doubts about the true value of Confederate money led to severe **inflation**, or price increases.

(Continues on the next page.)

Lesson Vocabulary

habeas corpus   a constitutional guarantee that no one can be held in prison without specific charges filed against them

draft law   an act of Congress giving the government authority to enlist men in the army without those men's consent

inflation   a general rise in the price of goods and services

Name _____ Class _____ Date _____

MODIFIED CORNELL NOTES

In the summer of 1863, Union General Ulysses S. Grant won several victories and split apart Confederate territory. In the East, Confederate troops were defeated in the Battle of Gettysburg. A few months later, President Lincoln gave a speech known as the Gettysburg Address, in which he reaffirmed the ideas that the Union was fighting for.

In 1864, Union General William T. Sherman led more than 60,000 troops on a 400-mile march of destruction through the South. The march was part of a strategy of **total war**, which targeted all the resources needed to support an army. On April 9, 1865, General Lee surrendered to General Grant.

In the North, the Civil War helped modernize society by encouraging agricultural and industrial growth. By contrast, the South was in shambles. Because most of the battles took place in the South, much of its agriculture was destroyed.

Even before the Civil War ended, Congress passed the Thirteenth Amendment, making slavery unconstitutional. For African Americans in the South, emancipation promised them new opportunities. Some joined the migration to the North and West looking for work while others remained in the South, hoping to work as **freedmen** on the land they had worked as slaves. The Thirteenth Amendment was a victory for the abolitionist movement and a milestone in the development of the civil rights movement in the nineteenth century.

Lesson Vocabulary

total war   a type of warfare in which all targets are attacked, including civilians and supply lines

freedman   former slaves who were now emancipated

Name _____ Class _____ Date _____

Answer the questions below using the information in the Lesson Summaries on the previous pages.

Lesson 1: Colonies and the Revolution

1. **Recognize Cause** What was the reason for the revolt of the 13 colonies against British rule?

They wanted self government

2. The belief in what type of rights influenced Thomas Jefferson as he wrote the Declaration of Independence?

life liberty, pursuit of happiness

Lesson 2: Founding a New Nation

3. **Recognize Sequence** Which constitution preceded the current United States Constitution?

4. What did the Federalists promise in order to secure ratification of the Constitution?

Lesson 3: America in the Early 1800s

5. How were the economies of the northern and southern states different in the early 1800s?

6. **Identify Main Ideas** How did the idea of Manifest Destiny influence expansionists?

Lesson 4: The Union in Crisis

7. What was popular sovereignty?

8. **Identify Causes and Effects** How did the split in the Democratic Party lead to Lincoln's victory in the 1860 election?

The north voted for him

REVIEW
TOPIC

Review Questions
CONNECTING WITH PAST LEARNINGS (continued)

Lesson 5: The Civil War

9. What was the significance of the Emancipation Proclamation?

_____

_____

10. Identify Detail Name the speech that President Lincoln gave that reaffirmed the ideas the Union was fighting for.

Cooper union

_____

_____

Name _____ Class _____ Date _____

Focus Question: What were the goals of Reconstruction? What actions were taken or events occurred that advanced or slowed down those goals? What final outcomes resulted from these actions and events?

As you read, focus on the positive and negative changes that occurred during Reconstruction and the impact they had. Identify the new laws and programs that began during Reconstruction. Assess the impact of Reconstruction in achieving its goals.

Goals	Actions/Events	Outcome
Return southern states to Union	• •	Southern states rejoin the Union.
	• • • • •	
	• • • • • •	

TOPIC 1
LESSON 1

Lesson Summary
PLANS FOR RECONSTRUCTION CLASH

MODIFIED CORNELL NOTES

During the era of Reconstruction (1865-1877), the federal government struggled with how to return the southern states to the Union, rebuild the South's ruined economy, and promote the rights of former slaves. Some argued that states should be allowed to rejoin the Union quickly with few conditions. But many claimed that the defeated states should first satisfy certain **stipulations**, such as swearing loyalty to the federal government and adopting state constitutions that guaranteed freedmen's rights.

President Lincoln wanted to readmit southern states as soon as ten percent of a state's voters took a loyalty oath to the Union. "Radical Republicans" in Congress opposed this plan, insisting that the Confederates had committed crimes. Congress passed the Wade-Davis Bill in 1864. It required a majority of a state's prewar voters to swear loyalty before the state could be readmitted, and it demanded full equality for African Americans. Lincoln killed the bill with a "pocket veto." However, he supported the Freedmen's Bureau. Its goal was to provide food, clothing, healthcare, and education for both black and white refugees in the South.

Lincoln's assassination in April 1865 thrust his Vice President, Andrew Johnson, into the presidency. Johnson wanted to restore the political status of the southern states as quickly as possible. He did not want African Americans to have the vote and had little sympathy for their plight. All the southern states instituted **black** codes, laws that limited the rights of African Americans. When Congress sought to overturn them by passing the Civil Rights Act of 1866, Johnson vetoed it.

(Continues on the next page.)

Lesson Vocabulary

stipulation   the act of specifying a condition in an argument
black codes   laws that restricted African Americans' rights and opportunities

TOPIC 1 — LESSON 1

Lesson Summary

PLANS FOR RECONSTRUCTION CLASH (continued)

MODIFIED CORNELL NOTES

Violence against African Americans in the South increased. To protect freedmen's rights, Congress passed the Fourteenth Amendment, which guaranteed equality under the law for all citizens. The Military Reconstruction Act of 1867 divided the South into five military districts and set requirements for states to reenter the Union. A power struggle between Congress and the President continued. The House of Representatives voted to **impeach** Johnson in 1868. He escaped being removed from office by one vote. In 1869, the Fifteenth Amendment was passed. It forbids any state from denying suffrage on the grounds of race or color.

Lesson Vocabulary

impeach   to accuse a public official of wrongdoing in office

MODIFIED CORNELL NOTES

TOPIC 1 LESSON 2

Lesson Summary
RECONSTRUCTION CHANGES THE SOUTH

The era of Reconstruction brought many changes to the South. Millions of southern African American men were now voters, and many served as elected officials. They used their voting power to usher the Republican Party into the South. The Republican Party attracted people who sought change and challenge. **Scalawags** were white men who had been locked out of pre-Civil War politics by their wealthier neighbors. They found allies in "**carpetbaggers**", or northern white or black men who relocated to the South.

Northern women, both white and black, had opportunities in the Reconstruction South that they could not pursue at home, including shaping the new public school system. Southerners opted for **segregation**, or separation of the races, in their school system. **Integration**—combining the schools—appealed to only the most radical white Republicans. Nevertheless, the beginning of a tax-supported public school system was a major Reconstruction success.

Many of the South's problems resulted from the uneven distribution of land. Wealth was defined by landownership. However, even owners of large tracts of land had no money with which to purchase supplies or pay workers. As a result, many southerners adopted one of three arrangements. Under the **sharecropping** system, a landowner dictated the crop and provided the sharecropper with a place to live and supplies in return for a "share" of the harvested crop. Under a **share-tenancy**, the farmworker chose what crop he would plant and bought his own supplies, then gave a share of the crop to the landowner. The most independent system was **tenant farming**, under which the tenant paid cash rent to the landowner and was free to choose his own crop and where to live.

(Continues on the next page.)

Lesson Vocabulary

scalawag   a negative term for a southern white person who supported the Republican Party after the Civil War

carpetbagger   a negative term for northerners who moved to the South after the Civil War

segregation   a forced separation, often by race

integration   the process of bringing together people of different races, religions, and social classes

sharecropping   a system in which a farmer tends to a portion of a planter's land in return for a share of the crop

share-tenancy   much like sharecropping, except that the farmer chooses what crop to plant and buys the supplies

tenant farming   a system in which a farmer paid rent to a landowner for the use of the land

Lesson Summary
RECONSTRUCTION CHANGES THE SOUTH (continued)

MODIFIED CORNELL NOTES

The more progress African Americans made, the more hostile white southerners became. Dozens of loosely organized groups of white southerners emerged to terrorize African Americans. The best known of these was the Ku Klux Klan. Racial violence grew even more widespread after the Fifteenth Amendment guaranteed all American men the right to vote. Congress took action, passing Enforcement Acts in 1870 and 1871. These acts made it a federal offense to interfere with a citizen's right to vote.

Name _____ Class _____ Date _____

MODIFIED CORNELL NOTES

The continued cost of military operations in the South worried many people. Beginning in 1871, troops were withdrawn from the South. In 1872, the Freedmen's Bureau was dissolved. The death of a Radical Republican leader in 1874 symbolized an important **transition**. A generation of white reformers, forged by abolitionist fervor, had passed away. Without such leaders, northern racial prejudice reemerged. In a series of landmark cases, the Supreme Court chipped away at African American freedom in the 1870s. A group of southern Democrats put together a coalition to return the South to the rule of white men. The main focus of their strategy was compromise: finding common issues that would unite white southerners with the goal of regaining power in Congress. These compromisers have become known as Redeemers.

In the 1876 election, the Democratic candidate received 51 percent of the popular vote. When the Republicans demanded a recount, they found enough mistakes to swing the election. Rutherford B. Hayes won by one electoral vote in what became known as the Compromise of 1877. In return, the remaining federal troops were withdrawn from the South and southern states were guaranteed federal subsidies to build railroads and improve their ports. Reconstruction was over. Although it fell short of its goals, Reconstruction opened new opportunities for African Americans in the North and South. Constitutional amendments provided hope for full inclusion in American society, although it would take generations to use them to gain racial equality.

Black southerners now had the right to vote. New opportunities opened up for them. Perhaps the most important goal was education. Hundreds of schools and dozens of teachers' colleges enabled African Americans to learn to read. However, some white southerners focused their own frustrations on trying to reverse the gains African Americans had achieved during Reconstruction. Groups such as the Ku Klux Klan used terror and violence to intimidate African Americans. Many African American freedoms were whittled away. Congress passed the Civil Rights Act of 1875 to guarantee black patrons the right to ride trains and use public facilities. However, the Supreme Court ruled that the decision about who could use public accommodations was a local issue to be governed by state or local laws. Southern municipalities took advantage of this ruling to further limit the rights of African Americans.

(Continues on the next page.)

Lesson Vocabulary

transition   the process of moving from one stage to another

TOPIC 1 LESSON 3

Lesson Summary
RECONSTRUCTION'S IMPACT (continued)

Even during the darkest days of Jim Crow, African Americans refused to accept their **status** as second-class citizens. They established black newspapers, women's clubs, fraternal organizations, schools and colleges, and political associations with the goal of securing their freedom. Former slave Ida B. Wells published the newspaper Free Speech. She wrote articles condemning the treatment of African Americans and criticizing lynching. Booker T. Washington argued that African Americans needed to accommodate themselves to segregation, build up economic resources, and establish reputations as hardworking and honest citizens. W.E.B. Du Bois criticized Washington and argued that African Americans should demand full and immediate equality.

Lesson Vocabulary

status   the legal position or condition of a person, group, country, etc.

TOPIC 1 Review Questions

Answer the questions below using the information in the Lesson Summaries on the previous pages.

Lesson 1: Plans for Reconstruction Clash

1. What were the main goals of the Reconstruction of the South?

End slavery, protect freed slaves, and general equality

2. Identify Main Ideas What did Congress do to protect the rights of African Americans?

13, 14, 15 amendments

Lesson 2: Reconstruction Changes the South

3. How did Republicans gain control of elected government in the South during Reconstruction?

4. Identify Main Ideas How did African Americans' lives change during Reconstruction?

They had more rights and were freed

Lesson 3: Reconstruction's Impact

5. What were some of the successes of Reconstruction?

6. Identify Main Ideas Why did many people in the North stop supporting Reconstruction?

Name _____ Class _____ Date _____

Note Taking Study Guide

INDUSTRY AND IMMIGRATION

Focus Question: As the "new immigrants" moved to the United States what issues did they face as newcomers? How did they deal with those issues?

As you read, focus upon the new setting immigrants to the U.S. faced during the late 1800s. Identify the national problems that would pose challenges to immigrants as well as the issues they confronted because of their immigrant status. Record how immigrants, workers, and other Americans responded to those challenges.

The Challenges	The Responses

MODIFIED CORNELL NOTES

Lesson Summary
INNOVATION BOOSTS GROWTH

The Civil War encouraged industrial growth by challenging industries to make products more quickly and efficiently than before. The country's growth was also fueled by its vast supply of natural resources. In addition, industries had a huge workforce to fuel growth. After the Civil War, many Europeans and some Asians immigrated to the United States.

Entrepreneurs fueled industrialization. Capitalism is a system in which individuals own most businesses. The heroes of this system are **entrepreneurs**, or people who invest money in a product or enterprise in order to make a profit.

Government encouraged the success of businesses in the late 1800s. To encourage the buying of American goods, Congress enacted **protective tariffs**, or taxes that would make imported goods cost more than those made locally. The government also adopted **laissez-faire** policies, which allowed businesses to operate under minimal government regulation.

Thomas Edison received more than 1,000 **patents** for new inventions. Edison and his team invented the light bulb. George Westinghouse developed technology to send electricity over long distances. Electricity lit streets and powered homes and factories. Alexander Graham Bell patented the telephone. By 1900, there were more than one million telephones in the United States.

To meet the growing demand for goods, factory owners developed a system known as **mass production**, which allowed them to turn out large numbers of products quickly and inexpensively.

(Continues on the next page.)

Lesson Vocabulary

entrepreneurs   people who build and manage businesses or enterprises in order to make a profit, often risking their own money or livelihoods

protective tariff   taxes on imported goods making the price high enough to protect domestic goods from foreign competition

laissez-faire   a theory advocating minimal government interference in the economy

patent   official rights given by the government to an inventor for the exclusive right to develop, use, and sell an invention for a set period of time

mass production   production of goods in large numbers through the use of machinery and assembly lines

MODIFIED CORNELL NOTES

While industry boomed in some parts of the United States, the South grew more slowly and lagged behind the rest of the country. Before the Civil War, the South had shipped its raw materials abroad or to the North for processing. After the war, the South first had to repair the damages of war and then attempt to catch up with the North's industrial development. In the 1880s, northern money helped the South build its own factories. Southern leaders called for a "New South" and encouraged the expansion of southern rail lines.

However, the South could not keep pace with the North in industrial growth. The South had plenty of natural resources, but it did not have enough skilled labor and capital investment. Wages were low and most of the region's wealth remained in the hands of a few people.

Before the Civil War, most southern planters had concentrated on cash crops, such as cotton and tobacco, which they grew to sell. Cotton remained the centerpiece of southern agriculture. However, many European textile factories had found other suppliers during the war, so the price of cotton had fallen. In the 1890s, the boll weevil struck at cotton crops across the South, causing cotton to continue to be an issue in the South as the 1900s began.

Industrialization touched every aspect of American life. Farms became mechanized. Mass production meant people had easier access to goods. As the United States grew as an economic power, it became more involved in the affairs of other nations.

Lesson Vocabulary

cash crop   crop grown for sale

TOPIC 2 LESSON 2

Lesson Summary
BIG BUSINESS RISES

To take advantage of larger markets, investors developed a form of group ownership known as a **corporation**. In a corporation, a number of people share ownership of a business. Corporations had access to huge amounts of money, allowing them to fund new technology or enter new industries.

Corporations worked to maximize profits in several ways. Some corporations tried to gain a **monopoly**, or complete control of a product or service. Other corporations worked to eliminate competition by forming **cartels**. In this arrangement, businesses making the same product agreed to limit their production and thus keep prices high. Another way to increase profits was to create a giant company with lower production costs. This system of consolidating many firms in the same business is called **horizontal integration**. John D. Rockefeller, Andrew Carnegie, and other businessmen also increased their power by gaining control of the many different business that make up all phases of a product's development. This process, called **vertical integration**, allowed businesses to reduce their costs and charge higher prices to competitors.

Consumers, workers, and the federal government gradually came to feel that systems like **trusts**, cartels, and monopolies gave powerful businesses an unfair advantage. At the same time, many people believed that business leaders served the nation positively. Factories, steel mills, and railroads provided jobs. The development of efficient business practices and industrialists' support for developing technology benefited the nation's economy and shaped the United States into a strong international leader. Finally, many business leaders were important philanthropists.

(Continues on the next page.)

Lesson Vocabulary

corporation   company recognized as a legal unit that has rights and liabilities separate from each of its members

monopoly   exclusive control by one company over an entire industry

cartel   association of producers of a good or service that prices and controls stocks in order to monopolize the market

horizontal integration   system of consolidating many firms in the same business

vertical integration   system of consolidating firms involved in all steps of a product's manufacture

trust   group of separate companies that are placed under the control of a single managing board in order to form a monopoly

TOPIC 2 LESSON 2

Lesson Summary
BIG BUSINESS RISES (continued)

Charles Darwin's theory of survival of the fittest was applied to the world of American capitalism and was called Social Darwinism. People used Social Darwinism to justify all sorts of beliefs and conditions, such as discrimination.

The federal government slowly became involved in regulating trusts. In 1890, the Senate passed the Sherman Antitrust Act. This act outlawed any trust that operated in restraint of trade or commerce among several states.

Lesson Summary
THE ORGANIZED LABOR MOVEMENT

MODIFIED CORNELL NOTES

Industrial growth produced wealth for business owners. However, some factory workers toiled long hours in dirty workhouses known as **sweatshops**. Many miners were forced to live in communities near their workplace. The housing in these **company towns** was owned by the business and rented to employees. By the time workers received wages, they owed most of their income to the company. As early as the 1820s, factory workers tried to gain more power against employers by using the technique of collective bargaining. One form of **collective bargaining** was the strike.

In the 1830s, a movement called socialism spread throughout Europe. Socialism is an economic and political philosophy that favors public, instead of private, control of property and income. Many labor activists borrowed ideas from socialism to support their goals.

The Knights of Labor, a labor union founded in 1869, included all workers of any trade, skilled or unskilled. The union sought broad social reform. In 1881, Terence V. Powderly became its leader.

In 1886, Samuel Gompers formed the American Federation of Labor (AFL). Unlike the Knights of Labor, the AFL focused on specific workers' issues, such as wages, working hours, and conditions.

On May 1, 1886, thousands of workers mounted a national demonstration for an eight-hour workday. Strikes erupted in several cities. At Haymarket Square in Chicago, frenzy broke out when a protester threw a bomb, killing a policeman. Dozens more people were killed. As a result of the Haymarket Riot, employers and many Americans associated union activities with violence.

The Homestead Strike was part of a wave of steelworkers' and miners' strikes that took place as economic depression crept across America. In each case, federal troops were called in.

In 1893, Eugene V. Debs, leader of the American Railway Union, called for a nationwide strike against the Pullman Company. By June 1894, nearly 300,000 railworkers had walked off their jobs. The Pullman Strike escalated, halting both railroad traffic and mail delivery. Federal troops were sent in to end the strike. Afterward, an important trend developed. The federal government regularly supported businesses over labor unions.

Lesson Vocabulary

sweatshop   small factories where employees have to work long hours under poor conditions for little pay

company town   communities in which residents rely upon one company for jobs, housing, and buying goods

collective bargaining   process in which employers negotiate with labor unions about hours, wages, and other working conditions

Lesson Summary
THE NEW IMMIGRANTS

MODIFIED CORNELL NOTES

Many early American immigrants were Protestants from northern and western Europe or German and Irish Catholics. Many were skilled, educated, and came as families to work on farms. In the 1870s, "new" immigrants from southern and eastern Europe came to America. They often came alone, were unskilled and poor, Catholic or Jewish, and settled in cities rather than on farms.

Two types of factors lead to immigration. Push factors compel people to leave their homes. These include famine, war, and persecution. Pull factors, such as economic opportunities or religious freedom, draw people to a new place. Land reform and low prices for grain pushed farmers in Mexico, Poland, China, and Italy to leave. Wars in China and eastern Europe, and religious persecution in eastern Europe were also push factors. Inexpensive land and employment opportunities were examples of pull factors.

Most immigrants traveled in **steerage**, the crowded and dirty lower decks of steamships. There, illness spread quickly. Ship owners did a preliminary medical screening before passengers boarded, but immigration officials still met ships at American ports to determine who could stay. Immigrants had to be healthy and prove that they had money, a skill, or a sponsor. Beginning in 1892, most European immigrants were processed at Ellis Island in New York Harbor. Chinese and other Asian immigrants were processed at Angel Island, which opened in 1910 in San Francisco Bay.

Volunteer organizations tried to help immigrants blend into the **"melting pot"** of American society. Still, many immigrants held on to their traditions. Newcomers often faced **nativism**, the belief that native-born white Americans were superior to newcomers. Immigrants competed for jobs and housing, and their religious and cultural differences made native-born Americans suspicious. Hostility toward Chinese laborers led Congress to pass the Chinese Exclusion Act in 1882, limiting the civil rights of Chinese immigrants and forbidding their naturalization. Despite opposition, immigrants fueled industrial growth, elected politicians, and made their traditions part of American culture.

Lesson Vocabulary

steerage   third-class accommodations on a steamship

"melting pot"   society in which people of different nationalities assimilate to form one culture

nativism   inclination to favor native inhabitants as opposed to immigrants

TOPIC
2
LESSON 5

Lesson Summary
A NATION OF CITIES

America went through **urbanization** in the late nineteenth century. The number of cities and their populations greatly increased. Major cities were clustered in the Northeast, on the Pacific Coast, and along Midwestern waterways. These centers of manufacturing and transportation were connected by new railroad lines.

In addition to immigrants looking for factory work, many rural-to-urban migrants moved to cities. Making a living by farming was increasingly difficult, and cities offered excitement and variety. Cities also offered great job possibilities for women. Children had the opportunity to attend school.

To meet increased demands for water, sewers, schools, and safety in growing cities, Americans developed new technologies. These innovations included electric trolleys, subways, and **skyscrapers**, tall buildings that housed large numbers of offices. Elisha Otis developed a safe elevator that would not fall if the lifting rope broke. Streetcars powered by electricity revolutionized transportation. **Mass transit**, public transportation systems capable of carrying a large number of people inexpensively, reshaped the nation. Those who could afford it moved to cleaner and quieter streetcar **suburbs** on the outskirts of cities and rode mass transit into the city for work and entertainment.

City planners created different zones for heavy industry, financial institutions, and residences. They also built public places, such as libraries, government buildings, universities, and parks. Landscape engineer Frederick Law Olmsted was hired to design a number of parks, including New York City's Central Park.

With the growth of cities came a number of problems. Cities were filthy and filled with trash. Most urban workers lived in overcrowded, low-cost multifamily housing called **tenements**. With few windows and little sanitation, they were unhealthy and dangerous places. Open fireplaces and gas lighting caused fires to quickly rip through cities. Unlit streets also posed dangers to those coming from or going to work. In response, many cities created firefighting teams and police forces. City planners began regulating housing, sanitation, and sewers.

Lesson Vocabulary

urbanization   expansion of cities and/or an increase in the number of people living in them

skyscrapers   very tall buildings

mass transit   public transportation systems that carry large numbers of people

suburbs   residential areas surrounding a city

tenements   multistory buildings divided into apartments to house as many residents as possible

Lesson Summary
NEW WAYS OF LIFE

MODIFIED CORNELL NOTES

In *The Gilded Age*, novelist Mark Twain depicted American society in the late 1800s as gilded, or having a rotten core but being covered with gold paint. Most Americans were not as cynical. More people worked for wages, and more products were available at lower prices, leading to a culture of **conspicuous consumerism**.

Department stores opened in the late 1850s. They used advertising to sell high-quality goods at fair prices. The postal service lowered shipping rates and offered free rural delivery, leading to a mail-order boom. Companies began creating trademarks with distinctive logos, and consumers began buying brand-name goods for the first time.

Transportation, advertising, and communication helped create a **mass culture** in which Americans became more and more alike in their consumption patterns. Household gadgets, toys, and food preferences were often the same from house to house. Newspapers both reflected and helped create mass culture, including Joseph Pulitzer's morning paper, the *World*. Pulitzer believed that newspapers should inform people and stir up controversy. William Randolph Hearst mimicked Pulitzer's sensationalist tactics in his newspaper, the *Morning Journal*. However, some novelists like Horatio Alger focused on moral issues. Ethnic and special-interest publications catered to urban dwellers, especially immigrants. Newspapers were successful, in part, because more people could read. Public education expanded rapidly, and by 1900, the literacy rate reached nearly 90 percent.

Urban areas became centers for new types of entertainment. Amusement parks were built close to cities around the country. Touring outdoor shows like "Buffalo Bill's Wild West Show" drew crowds. Religious-inspired entertainment, including the Chautauqua Circuit, also grew in popularity. **Vaudeville** shows, made up of musical drama, songs, and off-color comedy, were seen throughout the country. Movie theaters introduced motion pictures, charging a nickel for admission. Baseball, horse racing, bicycle racing, boxing, and football became popular spectator sports.

Lesson Vocabulary

conspicuous consumerism   purchasing of goods and services with the purpose of impressing others

mass culture   similar cultural patterns throughout a society as a result of the spread of transportation, communication, and advertising

vaudeville   type of show that included dancing, singing, and comedy sketches and became popular in the late nineteenth century

TOPIC 2 Review Questions
INDUSTRY AND IMMIGRATION

Answer the questions below using the information in the Lesson Summaries on the previous pages.

Lesson 1: Innovation Boosts Growth

1. What was the benefit of mass production?

_____

_____

2. **Identify Causes** How did entrepreneurs encourage industrialization?

_____

_____

Lesson 2: Big Business Rises

3. List two reasons some people had favorable opinions about the impact of big business.

_____

_____

4. **Identify Supporting Details** Name two methods that businesses used to increase their profits.

_____

_____

Lesson 3: The Organized Labor Movement

5. How did company towns negatively impact the workers who lived in them?

_____

_____

6. **Compare and Contrast** How did the goals of the Knights of Labor differ from those of the AFL?

_____

_____

Lesson 4: The New Immigrants

7. Describe the pull factors that drew immigrants to America.

_____

_____

8. **Identify Main Ideas** Discuss the challenges immigrants faced in America.

_____

_____

TOPIC 2 · Review Questions
INDUSTRY AND IMMIGRATION (continued)

Lesson 5: A Nation of Cities

9. Why did people move to cities?

_____

_____

10. **Identify Main Ideas** Describe the problems caused by rapid growth and the steps that cities took to solve them.

_____

_____

Lesson 6: New Ways of Life

11. Describe how a mass culture developed in America.

_____

_____

12. **Identify Main Ideas** What forms of entertainment were popular in the late 1800s?

_____

_____

TOPIC 3

Note Taking Study Guide

CHALLENGES IN THE LATE 1800s

Focus Question: What challenges did different ethnic groups face in the West?

The United States has always included many groups from many parts of the world. Sometimes there has been conflict between groups. As white settlers moved into the West, tensions flared with other groups. Fill in the graphic organizer to show at least two examples of the challenges faced by Native Americans, Mexican Americans, and Chinese Americans.

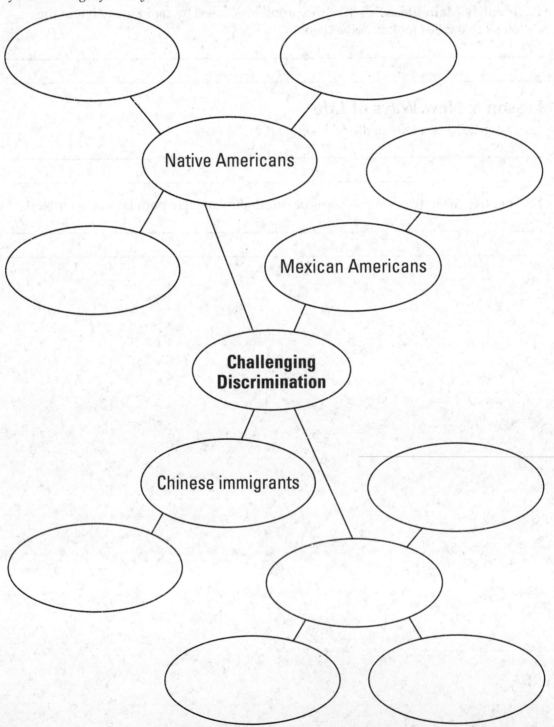

TOPIC 3 LESSON 1 — Lesson Summary
AMERICAN INDIANS UNDER PRESSURE

By the end of the Civil War, about 25,000 American Indians lived in the region west of the Mississippi River known as "The Great American Desert." Geography influenced cultural diversity, but all American Indian cultures saw themselves as part of nature and considered it sacred. By contrast, many whites viewed the land as a resource to produce wealth. In the early 1800s, the government began to move Native Americans out of the way of white settlers. Things changed when gold and silver were discovered in Indian Territory. In 1851, the government began to restrict American Indians to smaller areas. By the late 1860s, they were forced to live on **reservations**, where they lacked adequate resources.

In 1864, Colorado militia attacked an unarmed camp of Cheyenne and Arapaho. The Sand Creek Massacre, as it came to be known, spawned more warfare between Plains Indians and white settlers. When gold was discovered in the Black Hills, the Sioux, led by Chiefs Crazy Horse and Sitting Bull, tried to drive white prospectors out of Sioux lands. At the Battle of Little Big Horn in June 1876, the Sioux killed all the United States Army cavalry forces led by George Custer. In 1877, the Nez Percés tried to escape to Canada when the federal government wanted to relocate them to a smaller reservation. The Nez Percés were captured just short of the border and relocated to a barren reservation in Oklahoma. Their leader, Chief Joseph, traveled twice to Washington, D.C., to lobby for mercy for his people. In 1890, hostilities broke out at Wounded Knee, South Dakota, over a religious revival based on the Ghost Dance. The cavalry outgunned the Indians.

Policymakers hoped that American Indians would become farmers and **assimilate** into national life by adopting the culture and civilization of whites. In 1887, Congress passed the Dawes General Allotment Act. It replaced the reservation system with a system under which each American Indian family was granted a 160-acre farmstead. To help speed assimilation, missionaries and other reformers established boarding schools where Indian children were taught to live by the rules of white Americans.

Lesson Vocabulary

reservations   public lands where Native Americans were required to live by the federal government

assimilate   absorb into the main culture of a society

Name _____ Class _____ Date _____

MODIFIED CORNELL NOTES

Mining was the first great boom in the West. Mining camps sprang up quickly.

As industry in the West grew, the need for a **transcontinental railroad** linking the East and the West became apparent. Congress supported its construction in two ways: It provided money in the form of loans and made **land grants**, which gave builders wide stretches of land, alternating on each side of the track route. Work on the railroad began in 1863 and was completed in 1869. Railroads had far-reaching effects. They tied the nation together, moved products and people across the continent, and spurred industrial development. They also stimulated the growth of towns and cities and intensified the demand for American Indian land.

Cattle ranching was another western boom. With railroads capable of moving meat to eastern markets, the race was on for land and water. At first, cattle were raised on the **open-range** system. Property was not separated by fences, and cattle were branded for identification. Cowboys learned much from the Mexican vaqueros. By the mid-1880s, the heyday of open-range ranching came to an end.

The Great Plains was the last part of the country to be heavily settled by whites. Under the Homestead Act of 1862, the government offered farm plots to homesteaders. Some new settlers were formers slaves called "Exodusters." They followed an exodus out of bondage to a new "promised land" in Kansas and Oklahoma, where they planted crops and founded several all-black towns.

Chinese immigrants faced racial prejudice. Congress passed the Chinese Exclusion Act, prohibiting Chinese laborers from entering the country. Chinese "immigrants" turned to the federal courts. In 1898, the Supreme Court ruled that individuals of Chinese descent who were born in America could not be stripped of their citizenship.

Mexican Americans also struggled against discrimination. Despite guaranteed property rights, many Mexicans lost their lands after the Mexican-American War because they were unable to prove ownership. In the late 1880s and early 1890s, Las Gorras Blancas (the White Caps) fought back by engaging in guerilla warfare against the railroads and large ranchers.

Lesson Vocabulary

transcontinental railroad rail link between the eastern and the western United States

land grants land designated by the federal government for building schools, roads, or railroads

open-range method of ranching in which the rancher allowed his or her livestock to roam and graze over a vast area of grassland

Lesson Summary
CORRUPTION PLAGUES THE NATION

Inaction and political corruption characterized politics during the Gilded Age. Neither Democrats nor Republicans controlled the White House and both houses of Congress for more than two years in a row, making it difficult to pass new laws. Presidents during this era seemed weak and lacked integrity.

Political parties reached into nearly every ward and precinct in every city. Under the **spoils system**, politicians gave government jobs to loyal party workers without consideration of their qualifications. Government officials could and did use federal contracts to convince people to vote for their candidates.

A number of prominent figures promoted reforming the civil service system, a system that would include federal jobs in the executive branch. Under a reformed civil service, government workers would be offered jobs based on their expertise and keep those jobs regardless of which political party won the election. After President James Garfield was assassinated by a citizen who felt cheated out of a job, Vice President Chester Arthur signed the Pendleton Civil Service Act in 1883. This act established a **civil service** commission. The commission wrote an exam that all who sought government employment had to take before being hired. Getting a job was based on how well one did on the exam, not on one's political affiliation and connections.

Two economic issues created a political divide during the Gilded Age: the tariff and the monetary policy. Republicans favored a high tariff, arguing that it would promote job growth and allow American industry to grow. Democrats believed that high tariffs would raise prices and make it harder for American farmers to sell their goods abroad.

Disagreement flared over the gold standard, the use of gold as the basis of the nation's currency. Bankers and those in international trade feared the use of silver for money would undermine the economy. Farmers argued that the rejection of silver money would lead to declining prices and financial ruin. Congress passed the Coinage Act of 1873, which ended the minting of silver coins, but after protest, it authorized minting of silver dollars.

Lesson Vocabulary

political parties   a political party's organization that wins voter loyalty and guarantees power to a small group of leaders, who often abuse it for their own gain

spoils system   practice of the political party in power giving jobs and appointments to its supporters, rather than to people based on their qualifications

civil service   government departments and their non-elected employees

TOPIC 3 LESSON 4 — Lesson Summary
FARM ISSUES AND POPULISM

In the 1870s, Texas farmers began to organize and to **negotiate** as a group for lower prices for supplies. Local organizations joined to form the Farmers' Alliance. Alliance members tried to force railroads to lower freight prices. They also wanted the government to regulate the interest that banks could charge for loans.

Between 1870 and 1895, farm prices fell sharply. At the same time, the cost of doing business increased. Many farmers **mortgaged** their farms to survive. Farmers blamed big business, especially the railroads and banks, for their problems. They believed that railroads charged whatever rates they wanted and that banks set interest rates too high.

In 1867, Oliver H. Kelley, a Minnesota farmer and businessman, organized the Grange, an organization of farmers that grew to nearly a million members. It was one of a network of organizations created to solve farmers' problems. The Grange provided education and called for the regulation of railroad and **grain elevator** rates. Grangers also prompted the federal government to establish the Interstate Commerce Commission (ICC) to oversee interstate transportation.

Farmers' Alliances took up the call for reform in the late 1870s. They formed cooperatives to collectively sell crops and called on the federal government to establish "sub-treasuries," or postal banks, to provide farmers with low-interest loans.

The spread of the Farmers' Alliances culminated with the creation of the Populist Party, or People's Party, in 1892. The party grew rapidly, putting pressure on the two major political parties to consider their demands. They called for the coinage of silver, or **"free silver,"** to fight low prices. To combat high costs, they demanded government ownership of railroads. In the 1892 election, the Populists elected several governors and senators, and 10 members of Congress. Their presidential candidate received more than one million votes.

Following this success, Populists were forced to decide whether to nominate their own presidential candidate or to endorse Democratic Party nominee William Jennings Bryan for the 1896 election. They chose to endorse Bryan, who supported many Populist proposals.

Bryan lost the election to Republican candidate William McKinley, partly because his emphasis on monetary reform, especially free silver, did not appeal to urban workers. The Populist decision to endorse Bryan weakened the party at the local and state levels. The party never recovered, and by the early 1900s, it had disappeared as a viable alternative to the two major political parties.

Lesson Vocabulary

negotiate   to arrange or bring about a settlement of a matter

mortgage   to borrow money against a piece of property by a legal agreement against a piece of property

grain elevator   a building for storing grain

free silver   a monetary policy that linked the supply of U.S. dollars to silver rather than gold

TOPIC 3

Review Questions

CHALLENGES IN THE LATE 1800s

Answer the questions below using the information in the Lesson Summaries on the previous pages.

Lesson 1: American Indians Under Pressure

1. Who was Chief Joseph?

_____

_____

2. Recognize Sequence How did life change for Native Americans after gold and silver were discovered in Indian Territory?

_____

_____

Lesson 2: The West Is Transformed

3. Who were the Exodusters?

_____

_____

4. Identify Main Ideas Why were early settlers attracted to the West?

_____

_____

Lesson 3: Corruption Plagues the Nation

5. What is the term for the use of gold as a nation's currency?

_____

_____

6. Identify Main Ideas Discuss two economic issues that were important to politics during the Gilded Age.

_____

_____

_____

Lesson 4: Farm Issues and Populism

7. What candidate did Populists endorse in the 1896 presidential election?

_____

_____

8. Identify Causes and Effects Describe the problems that led farmers to create groups such as the Grange.

_____

_____

_____

TOPIC
4

Note Taking Study Guide

AMERICA COMES OF AGE

Focus Question: What specific areas of American life did Progressives believe needed to be reformed and how did they want to solve those problems?

As you read, focus upon the problems that Progressives recognized and their solutions to those problems.

Problem	Solution

TOPIC 4 — LESSON 1

Lesson Summary
PROGRESSIVES DRIVE REFORM

Industrialization, urbanization, and immigration brought many benefits to America, but they also produced challenging social problems. Progressivism was a social movement that arose in the 1890s to tackle these problems. Journalists whose stories dramatized the need for reform were called **muckrakers**. One leading muckraker was Lincoln Steffens, a magazine editor who published stories about political corruption. Another was Jacob Riis, a photographer whose pictures revealed life in urban slums. Novelist Frank Norris showed how the Southern Pacific Railroad kept a stranglehold on California farmers in *The Octopus*. Upton Sinclair's novel *The Jungle* revealed the unsafe and unsanitary conditions of Chicago meatpacking plants.

The work of the muckrakers increased popular support for progressivism and helped the Progressives bring about reforms. Laws were passed to end child labor and break up monopolies and trusts. After a fire at a garment factory killed nearly 150 workers, Progressives were able to get laws passed to protect worker safety.

Many reformers thought that Christianity should be the basis of social reform. These followers of the Social Gospel believed that society would improve if people followed the Bible's teachings about charity and justice. One form of charity was the **settlement house**, which offered services for the poor such as child care and classes in English. Hull House in Chicago was a famous settlement house founded by Jane Addams. Her work inspired others to help solve the problems of the urban poor by becoming social workers.

(Continues on the next page.)

Lesson Vocabulary

muckraker   writer who uncovers and exposes misconduct in government or business

settlement house   community center organized at the turn of the twentieth century to provide social services to the urban poor

Name _____ Class _____ Date _____

Lesson Summary
PROGRESSIVES DRIVE REFORM (continued)

MODIFIED CORNELL NOTES

In order to reform politics and remove corrupt governments, Progressives pushed for a number of new laws. Dynamic leaders such as Wisconsin Governor Robert La Follette created tools to limit the power of political bosses and business interests. Reformers created the **direct primary** so citizens, not political bosses, could select nominees for upcoming elections. The **initiative** gave people the power to put a proposed new law directly on the ballot. The **referendum** allowed citizens to approve or reject laws passed by a legislature. The **recall** gave voters the power to remove elected officials from office before their terms ended. These reforms brought about by Progressives continue to affect society today.

Lesson Vocabulary

direct primary   election in which citizens themselves vote to select nominees for upcoming elections

initiative   process in which citizens put a proposed new law directly on the ballot

referendum   process that allows citizens to approve or reject a law passed by a legislature

recall   process by which voters can remove elected officials from office before their term ends

Lesson Summary
WOMEN GAIN RIGHTS

MODIFIED CORNELL NOTES

In the early 1900s, a growing number of women sought to do more than fulfill their roles as wives and mothers. Many went to college to prepare for careers in teaching and nursing. Women had already won a shorter workday, but reformers saw the need for more changes. Florence Kelley believed that unfair prices for household goods hurt women and their families, so she helped found the National Consumers League (NCL). The NCL labeled products made in safe workplaces. The NCL also asked the government to improve food and workplace safety and assist the underemployed.

Women continued to fight for the right to vote, to own property, and to receive an education. Although women failed to gain the vote, the number of women attending college jumped dramatically.

Women also sought changes in the home. With the **temperance movement**, led by the Women's Christian Temperance Union (WCTU), women tried to reduce or end the consumption of alcohol. Members of the WCTU blamed alcohol for some men's abuse and neglect of their families. Margaret Sanger sought a different change. She thought that family life and women's health would improve if mothers had fewer children. Sanger opened the nation's first birth-control clinic. Ida B. Wells established the National Association of Colored Women, which helped African American families by providing childcare and education.

One of progressivism's boldest goals was women's **suffrage**, or the right to vote. This fight was started in the 1860s but was re-energized by Carrie Chapman Catt in the 1890s. Catt toured the country encouraging women to join the National American Woman Suffrage Association (NAWSA). This group lobbied Congress for the right to vote and used the referendum process to try to get women the vote in several states. By 1918, this strategy had helped women get the vote in several states. Alice Paul was more vocal in her efforts. In 1917, she formed the National Women's Party (NWP), which staged protest marches and hunger strikes and even picketed the White House to demand the right to vote. When the United States entered World War I in 1917, the NAWSA supported the war effort. Its actions and those of the NWP convinced a growing number of legislators to support a women's suffrage amendment. This reform became official in 1920 as the Nineteenth Amendment. Women finally had the right to vote for President.

Lesson Vocabulary

temperance movement   movement aimed at stopping alcohol abuse and the problems created by it

suffrage   the right to vote

Lesson Summary
STRIVING FOR EQUALITY

MODIFIED CORNELL NOTES

The Progressive Era was not so progressive for nonwhite and immigrant Americans. Most Progressives were white Anglo-Saxon Protestant reformers who were indifferent or hostile to minorities.

Settlement houses and other civic groups played a big role in the **Americanization** efforts of many Progressives. Americanization occurred when Progressives encouraged everyone to follow white, middle-class ways of life.

Many Progressives shared the same prejudices against non-whites as other Americans. They agreed with so-called scientific theories that said that dark-skinned peoples had less intelligence than whites. They also supported segregation, or separation of the races, and laws to limit minority voting.

African American reformers responded in different ways to formal segregation and discrimination. For example, Booker T. Washington told blacks that the best way to win their rights was to be patient and to earn the respect of white Americans. W.E.B. Du Bois, on the other hand, said that blacks should demand immediately all the rights guaranteed by the Constitution.

W.E.B. Du Bois was a member of the Niagara Movement, a group that called for rapid progress and more education for blacks. After a race riot broke out in Illinois, its members joined with white reformers to form the National Association for the Advancement of Colored People (NAACP). The NAACP planned to use the court system to fight for the civil rights of African Americans, including the right to vote. The efforts of the NAACP mostly helped middle-class blacks, but the Urban League focused on poorer urban workers. It helped families buy clothes and books and helped factory workers and maids find jobs.

African Americans were not alone in seeking their rights. Individuals and organizations of diverse ethnic groups spoke out against injustice and created self-help agencies. Jews in New York City formed the Anti-Defamation League to defend themselves against verbal attacks and false statements. Mexican Americans in several states formed **mutualistas**, groups that gave loans and provided legal assistance to the poor.

Lesson Vocabulary

Americanization   belief that assimilating immigrants into American society would make them more loyal citizens

mutualistas   organized groups of Mexican Americans that make loans and provide legal assistance to other members of their community

TOPIC 4
LESSON 4

Lesson Summary
REFORMERS IN THE WHITE HOUSE

MODIFIED CORNELL NOTES

Theodore Roosevelt was a war hero, seasoned politician, and a dedicated reformer when he became President in 1901. Roosevelt used the power of the federal government to take on big business, breaking up **trusts** he considered abusive. In 1906, Roosevelt convinced Congress to pass the Hepburn Act, which limited what railroads could charge for shipping.

Roosevelt put millions of acres of forests under federal control. Like the head of the Division of Forestry, Gifford Pinchot, Roosevelt believed in the "rational use" of forests. The forests would be protected as future sources of lumber. To help settle fights over sources of water in the West, Roosevelt pushed for passage of the National Reclamation Act. That law gave the government power to build and manage dams to control where and how water was used.

After two terms in office, Roosevelt wanted William Howard Taft to follow him. However, Taft did not follow the course Roosevelt had set, and Roosevelt became disappointed and, later, angry. He began to speak out against Taft, promoting what he called New Nationalism, a program to restore the government's trust-busting power. A group of Progressives created the Progressive Party and nominated Roosevelt as its candidate for President.

During the 1912 election, Roosevelt and Taft split the Republican Party vote, allowing Democrat Woodrow Wilson to win the election. Like Roosevelt, Wilson was a reformer who thought government should play an active role in the economy. He shaped his ideas into a three-part program he called the New Freedom.

First, Wilson tried to prevent manufacturers from charging unfairly high prices. He cut **tariffs** on imported goods, which made foreign goods more competitive in the United States and forced U.S. producers to charge fair prices.

Second, Wilson pushed Congress to pass the Federal Reserve Act. This law gave the government authority to supervise banks by placing national banks under the control of the Federal Reserve Board.

(Continues on the next page.)

Lesson Vocabulary

trust   a combination of businesses formed to reduce competition

tariff   a tax on imported or exported goods

Third, Wilson made sure that trusts did not behave unfairly. He persuaded Congress to create the Federal Trade Commission (FTC) to monitor business practices and stop false advertising and dishonest labeling.

Progressivism had a major impact on the nation. Political reforms expanded the power of voters. Economic reforms enabled the government to **regulate** corporations and banks in the interest of the public. **Consumer** protections gave the public confidence that the products they bought were not harmful. The government also began to manage natural resources all over the nation.

Lesson Vocabulary

regulate to make rules or laws to govern or control

consumer a person who buys and uses goods and services

TOPIC 4
LESSON 5
Lesson Summary
AMERICAN INFLUENCE GROWS

During the late 1800s, the United States began to acquire influence and territory outside of its continental borders. It pursued a policy of **imperialism**, or the use of economic, political, and military control over weaker territories. Many imperialist nations wanted colonies to serve as **extractive economies**. Raw materials would be removed from these colonies and sent to the home country. In America there was a surplus of goods. American industrialists would benefit because they could sell their commodities in new colonial markets around the world.

Alfred T. Mahan, a historian and officer in the United States Navy, called upon the government to build a large navy in order to protect American interests around the world. To justify imperialism, many imperialists used ideas of racial, national, and cultural superiority. One of these ideas was Social Darwinism, the belief that life is a competitive struggle and that some races are superior to others and more fit to rule. Historian Frederick J. Turner wrote that America needed a large amount of unsettled land to succeed. Some Americans felt that the nation should expand into foreign lands.

In 1853, Commodore Matthew Perry sailed a large naval force to Japan. Perry won the Japanese emperor's favor by showering him with lavish gifts. Within a year, Japan agreed to trade with the United States. In 1867, Secretary of State William Seward bought Alaska from Russia. The purchase almost doubled the size of the United States and provided timber, oil, and other natural resources. In Latin America, U.S. business owners sought to expand their trade and investments, which increased the U.S. sphere of influence.

The Hawaiian Islands had been economically linked to the United States for almost a century. American sugar planters owned much of Hawaiian land. They used their influence to exclude many Hawaiians from the voting process. Queen Liliuokalani, the ruler of Hawaii, tried to limit the political power of the white minority. In 1893, the planters overthrew the queen and set up a new government. The United States annexed Hawaii in 1898. The United States was abandoning isolationism and emerging as a new power on the global stage.

Lesson Vocabulary

imperialism   political, military, and economic domination of strong nations over weaker territories

extractive economies   economy in a colony where the colonizing country removed raw materials and shipped them back home to benefit its own economy

MODIFIED CORNELL NOTES

At the end of the nineteenth century, tensions were rising between Spain and its colony in Cuba. Cuban patriot **José Martí** launched a war for independence from Spain in 1895. Many Americans supported the Cubans, whose struggle for freedom and democracy reminded Americans of their own struggle for independence.

Newspaper publishers Joseph Pulitzer and William Randolph Hearst heightened the public's dislike of the Spanish government. Their publications, known as the Yellow Press, pushed for war with Spain by printing exaggerated stories of Spanish atrocities. In February 1898, Hearst's *New York Journal* published a letter written by Spain's ambassador, which called McKinley a weak and stupid politician. The letter fueled American **jingoism**, or aggressive nationalism. Soon after, the American battleship *Maine* exploded in Havana harbor. The Yellow Press promptly accused Spain of blowing up the battleship. In April 1898, the U.S. Congress declared war on Spain, beginning the Spanish-American War.

In the Spanish-held Philippines, Commodore George Dewey quickly destroyed a large part of the Spanish fleet. While Dewey was defeating the Spanish navy, Filipino nationalists led by Emilio Aguinaldo were defeating the Spanish army. In August, Spanish troops surrendered to the United States.

Meanwhile, U.S. troops landed in Cuba in June 1898. Although the troops were poorly trained, wore unsuitable uniforms, and carried old, outdated weapons, they were successful. Spanish forces in Cuba surrendered to the United States. Future President Theodore Roosevelt organized a force known as the Rough Riders. Joined by African American soldiers from the Ninth and Tenth Cavalry regiments, the Rough Riders played a key role in the war.

In December 1898, Spain and the United States signed the Treaty of Paris, officially ending the Spanish-American War. Spain gave up control of Cuba, Puerto Rico, and the Pacific island of Guam. It also sold the Philippines to the United States.

During the Spanish-American War, Filipino nationalist Emilio Aguinaldo viewed America as an ally in the Filipino struggle for independence. However, when the United States kept possession of the Philippines after the war, Aguinaldo grew disillusioned. He helped organize an **insurrection**, or rebellion, against U.S. rule.

The Filipino insurgents relied on **guerrilla warfare** tactics, including surprise raids and hit-and-run attacks. In turn, the U.S. military used extraordinary measures to crush the rebellion. The war in the Philippines highlighted the rigors of fighting against guerilla insurgents. Nearly 5,000 Americans and 200,000 Filipinos were killed in the fighting.

Lesson Vocabulary

jingoism   aggressive nationalism; support for warlike foreign policy

insurrection   rebellion

guerrilla warfare   nontraditional combat methods

TOPIC 4 — LESSON 7

Lesson Summary
THE UNITED STATES EMERGES AS A WORLD POWER

The United States also wanted to increase trade with China. By 1899, Britain, France, Germany, and Russia had carved China into distinct **spheres of influence**, or zones. Because the United States did not have a zone, this system of privileged access to Chinese markets threatened to limit American trade. U.S. Secretary of State John Hay made it clear that America demanded equal trade access.

In May 1900, a Chinese nationalist group launched the Boxer Rebellion in objection to the presence of foreigners. As the rebellion engulfed China, Secretary of State Hay reasserted America's Open Door Policy, which stated that the United States wanted free trade, not colonies, in China. A multinational force of European, American, and Japanese troops put down the uprising.

In 1905, President Roosevelt negotiated an end to the Russo-Japanese War. The President's intervention displayed America's growing role in world affairs.

Roosevelt promoted military preparedness to protect U.S. interests in Asia. In 1907, Roosevelt sent a force of navy ships, known as the Great White Fleet, on a cruise around the world to demonstrate America's increased military power.

After the Spanish-American War, the United States assumed control of Puerto Rico and Cuba. In 1900, the U.S. Congress passed the **Foraker Act**, which established a civil government in Puerto Rico. In 1917, Puerto Ricans gained more citizenship rights and greater control over their own legislature.

After assuming the presidency, Theodore Roosevelt promoted **"big stick" diplomacy**, which relied on a strong U.S. military to achieve America's goals. Roosevelt used this forceful approach to intimidate Colombia and gain control over the "Canal Zone" in Panama. America then built the Panama Canal, a waterway that connected the Atlantic and Pacific oceans.

In 1913, President Woodrow Wilson, who had criticized imperialism, promoted his policy of **"moral diplomacy."** Wilson promised that America would work to promote "human rights, national integrity, and opportunity."

Although he intended to take U.S. policy in a different direction, President Wilson nevertheless used the military on a number of occasions.

Lesson Vocabulary

spheres of influence   a region dominated and controlled by an outside power

"big stick" diplomacy   Theodore Roosevelt's policy of creating and using, when necessary, a strong military to achieve America's goals

"moral diplomacy"   Woodrow Wilson's statement that the U.S. would not use force to assert influence in the world, but would instead work to promote human rights

Answer the questions below using the information in the Lesson Summaries on the previous pages.

Lesson 1: Progressives Drive Reform

1. How did settlement houses help the poor?

_____

_____

2. Identify Details List four muckrakers whose work in the 1890s helped increase the public's awareness about social and political problems, and describe their work.

_____

_____

Lesson 2: Women Gain Rights

3. What methods did reformers use to fight for women's suffrage?

_____

_____

4. Identify Main Ideas What goal did Margaret Sanger, Ida B. Wells, and Florence Kelley share?

_____

_____

Lesson 3: Striving for Equality

5. Why did Progressives not fight for the civil rights of minorities?

_____

_____

6. Main Idea and Details How did Booker T. Washington differ from W.E.B. Du Bois in his approach to civil rights?

_____

_____

Lesson 4: Reformers in the White House

7. Why did President Roosevelt and Gifford Pinchot want to protect forests?

_____

_____

8. Identify Main Ideas How were the Square Deal and the New Nationalism programs similar?

_____

_____

TOPIC 4 Review Questions
AMERICA COMES OF AGE (continued)

Lesson 5: American Influence Grows

9. How did Social Darwinism contribute to imperialism?

_____

_____

10. **Identify Causes** What led to the annexation of Hawaii?

_____

_____

Lesson 6: The Spanish-American War

11. What territories did Spain give up in the Treaty of Paris?

_____

_____

12. **Identify Causes and Effects** What was the effect of the Yellow Press on the American public?

_____

_____

Lesson 7: The United States Emerges as a World Power

13. What was the purpose of proclaiming the Open Door Policy?

_____

_____

14. **Recognize Sequence** Number the following events in chronological order: Great White Fleet sails; China carved into spheres of influence; Roosevelt negotiates "Gentlemen's Agreement"

_____

_____

Name _____ Class _____ Date _____

Focus Question: What toll did America's involvement in World War I take on various aspects of society?

As you read, note specific examples that support the idea that the Economy, Women, Soldiers, and Politics were all greatly impacted by American involvement in World War I.

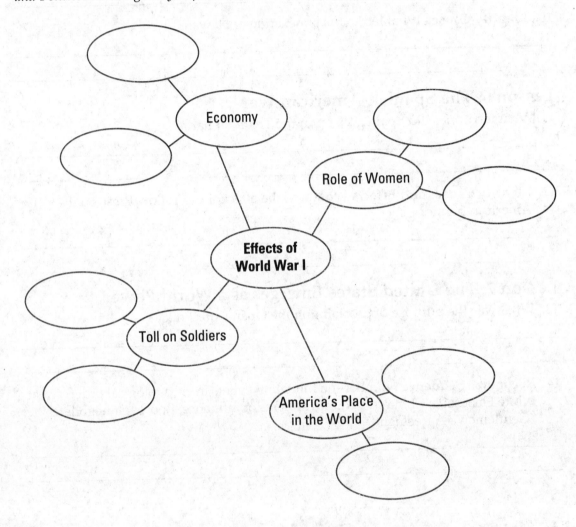

TOPIC 5 LESSON 1 — Lesson Summary
AMERICA ENTERS WORLD WAR I

Although there had been no major wars, the 50 years before World War I were not tranquil. Nationalism renewed old grudges among countries. **Militarism**, or glorification of the military, eventually produced an arms race between Germany and Britain at sea and among Germany, France, and Russia on land.

In addition to strengthening their military power, European leaders prepared for war by forming alliances. Germany, Austria-Hungary, and Italy formed the Triple Alliance. Opposing them were France, Russia, and Great Britain, which formed the Triple Entente. In 1914, a Serbian youth assassinated Francis Ferdinand, the archduke of Austria-Hungary. War spread as European countries entered the fighting to help their allies. Russia came to the aid of Serbia against Austria. Germany declared war on Russia. France, Russia's ally, declared war on Germany. After Germany declared war on Belgium, Great Britain declared war on Germany. World War I had begun.

Although fighting went on in Eastern Europe, the Middle East, and other parts of the world, the Western Front in France became the critical battle front. German soldiers settled onto high ground, dug trenches, and fortified their position. The French and British then dug their own trenches. A stalemate developed and the war dragged on for years. New military technology, including machine guns and poison gas, led to millions of **casualties**.

As the war continued in Europe, President Woodrow Wilson called for Americans to remain impartial. However, Germany's brutal invasion of Belgium swayed American opinion against Germany. Americans also protested when a German submarine, or **U-boat**, sank the British passenger liner Lusitania.

In January 1917, German Foreign Minister Arthur Zimmermann sent a telegram to Mexico proposing an alliance between Germany and Mexico. The Zimmermann note was intercepted by the British, who gave it to American authorities. When the telegram was published, Americans were shocked by its contents. Next, Germany announced unrestricted submarine warfare against Britain. On April 6, 1917, the U.S. Congress declared war on Germany.

Lesson Vocabulary

militarism   glorification of the military.

casualties   soldiers killed, wounded, or missing

U-boat   German submarine

Name _____ Class _____ Date _____

MODIFIED CORNELL NOTES

When the United States entered World War I, its army was only a fraction of the size of European armies. To build the army, Congress passed the Selective Service Act, which authorized a draft of young men for military service in Europe.

While the Selective Service Commission raised an army, the War Industries Board (WIB), headed by Bernard Baruch, regulated all industries engaged in the war effort. The WIB also urged Americans to conserve food as a patriotic gesture. As head of the Food Administration, future President Herbert Hoover set high prices for food to encourage farmers to increase production.

In 1917, many Americans questioned U.S. involvement in the war. The Committee on Public Information (CPI) worked to convince the American public that the war effort was a just cause. George Creel, the director of the CPI, combined education with a widespread advertising campaign to "sell America."

Still, not all Americans favored America's entry into the war. German and Irish Americans tended to oppose the Allies. Opposition also came from **conscientious objectors**, people whose moral or religious beliefs forbade them to fight in wars.

During the war, the U.S. government restricted individual rights. In June 1917, Congress passed the Espionage Act, which banned subversive newspapers, magazines, or printed materials on the grounds that they were forms of **espionage**. Congress further limited freedom of speech with the Sedition Act. In *Schenck* v. *United States* (1919), the Supreme Court ruled that there are times when the First Amendment protections on speech do not apply.

The war also brought substantial social changes. It created jobs for women while men were serving in the military and ushered in the Nineteenth Amendment, which gave women the right to vote. Meanwhile, many African Americans from the rural South were moving to the industrial North. The Great Migration saw more than 1.2 million African Americans move to the North to escape racism and find better jobs. Many Mexicans also sought to improve their lives. Some crossed the border into the United States in search of jobs. World War I had opened up new opportunities for women, African Americans, and Mexican Americans.

Lesson Vocabulary

conscientious objectors   person whose moral or religious beliefs forbid him or her to fight in wars

espionage   disloyal or treasonable activities

Lesson Summary
THE END OF WORLD WAR I

MODIFIED CORNELL NOTES

When the United States entered World War I in 1917, the conflict had become a deadly stalemate. Hoping to end the conflict before the Americans could make a difference, Germany renewed unrestricted submarine warfare. British and American convoys provided mutual safety by sending warships to protect merchant ships. As a result, shipping losses from U-boat attacks fell sharply.

In November 1917, radical communists led by Vladimir Lenin gained control of Russia. Fighting stopped between Russia and Germany, which allowed Germany to launch an all-out offensive on the Western Front. American troops under the command of John J. Pershing helped stop the German offensive and launch successful counterattacks. On November 11, 1918, Germany surrendered, officially ending World War I.

In what became known as the Fourteen Points, President Woodrow Wilson promoted openness, encouraged independence, and supported freedom. Wilson also advocated **self-determination**, or the right of people to choose their own form of government. Finally, he asked to form the League of Nations, a world organization where countries could gather and peacefully resolve their quarrels.

In 1919, the victorious Allies held a peace conference in France. Although Wilson's hope for the League of Nations was fulfilled, the various peace treaties created almost as many problems as they solved. The other Allied leaders insisted that Germany make **reparations**, or payment for war damages. When the map of Europe was redrawn, national self-determination was violated many times.

In the United States, many people opposed the treaty. A handful of senators known as the **"irreconcilables"** believed that the United States should not entangle itself in world organizations such as the League of Nations. A larger group of senators, led by Henry Cabot Lodge and known as **"reservationists,"** opposed the treaty as it was written. Wilson and his opponents refused to put aside their differences and compromise, and the Senate did not ratify the treaty. Without full American support, the League of Nations proved unable to maintain peace among nations.

Lesson Vocabulary

self-determination   the right of people to choose their own form of government

reparations   payment for war damages

"irreconcilables"   isolationist senators who oppose any treaty ending World War I that had a League of Nations folded into it

"reservationists"   group of U.S. senators who were prepared to vote for the Treaty of Versailles as long as some changes were made to it

TOPIC 5 LESSON 4

Lesson Summary
THE POSTWAR ECONOMY BOOMS

The end of the war meant the end of wartime economic opportunities for women and African Americans. Adding to this crisis atmosphere were normal postwar adjustments. Falling agricultural prices made it difficult for farmers to pay their debts. **Inflation**, or rising prices, meant industrial workers' wages did not buy as much as they had bought during the war.

By 1920, the United States was the richest, most industrialized country in the world. The United States was also the largest **creditor nation** in the world, meaning that other countries owed the United States more money than the United States owed them. As a result of World War I, America's economic and political standing in the world had fundamentally changed.

During the 1920s, revolutionary **mass-production** techniques enabled American workers to produce more goods in less time. Because of this, the economy boomed. The automobile industry played a major role in the boom. Carmaker Henry Ford introduced new methods and ideas that changed the way manufactured goods were made. Ford also hired **scientific management** experts to improve his **assembly line** for the mass production of automobiles. In two years, the time it took to build an automobile dropped from more than 12 hours to just 90 minutes. This made the Model T affordable for most Americans, and automobile ownership skyrocketed.

(Continues on the next page.)

Lesson Vocabulary

inflation   rising prices

creditor nation   country which is owed more money by other countries than it owes other countries

mass-production   production of goods in large numbers through the use of machinery and assembly lines

scientific management   theory of management that studies how work is done with the goal of improving efficiency

assembly line   arrangement of equipment and workers in which work passes from operation to operation in direct line until the product is assembled

TOPIC 5 / LESSON 4

Lesson Summary
THE POSTWAR ECONOMY BOOMS (continued)

A flood of new, affordable goods became available to the public, creating a **consumer revolution**. At the same time, a new kind of credit called **installment buying** enabled consumers to buy goods they otherwise could not have afforded. Buyers made a small down payment on a product and paid the rest in monthly installments.

Americans were also buying stock on credit. As stock prices soared in a **bull market**, people began **buying on margin**, paying as little as 10 percent of the stock price upfront to a broker. If the stock price rose, the buyer could pay off the broker and still make a profit. If the price fell, the buyer still owed the broker the full price of the stock.

The economic boom was felt more in cities, where jobs were plentiful, than in rural areas. As cities grew, people moved out to suburbs and drove their new automobiles into the city to work.

Lesson Vocabulary

consumer revolution   flood of new, affordable goods in the decades after World War I

installment buying   method of purchase in which buyer makes a small down payment and then pays off the rest of the debt in regular monthly payments

bull market   period of rising stock prices

buying on margin   system of buying stocks in which a buyer pays a small percentage of the purchase price while the broker advances the rest

TOPIC 5 LESSON 5

Lesson Summary

GOVERNMENT IN THE 1920s

In 1920, fun-loving Warren G. Harding was elected President. Preferring a laissez-faire approach to business, Harding named banker Andrew Mellon as Secretary of the Treasury. Together they worked to reduce regulations on businesses and to raise protective tariff rates. This made it easier for U.S. producers to sell goods at home. In response, Europeans also raised tariffs, making U.S. products more expensive there. Laws had been previously passed to break up monopolies and protect workers, but Harding favored less restriction on businesses. Secretary of Commerce Herbert Hoover asked business leaders to voluntarily make advancements.

Harding admitted that he preferred playing golf or poker to governing. He trusted his friends with important government positions. One friend, Charles Forbes, wasted millions of dollars while running the Veterans' Bureau. Another, Secretary of the Interior Albert Fall, created the biggest **scandal** of Harding's administration. In the Teapot Dome scandal, Fall took **bribes** to transfer control of oil reserves from the United States Navy to private oilmen. Fall was later forced to return the oil and sentenced to a year in jail. Harding died in 1923, before the full extent of the scandal came to light.

The new President, Calvin Coolidge, was quiet and honest. He put his administration in the hands of men who held to the simple **virtues** of an older generation. Like Harding, he mistrusted the use of legislation to achieve social change. He favored big business. He reduced the national debt and lowered taxes to give incentives to businesses. However, Coolidge said and did nothing about many of the country's problems, such as low prices for farm crops, racial discrimination, and low wages.

In foreign policy, Coolidge pushed European governments to repay war debts to the United States. In 1924, an agreement known as the Dawes Plan was arranged to help Germany, France, and Great Britain repay those debts. In 1928, exhausted by World War I, 62 nations signed the Kellogg-Briand Pact, a treaty that outlawed war. Unfortunately, there was no way for nations to enforce the treaty, and it was quickly forgotten.

Lesson Vocabulary

scandal an event involving immoral or illegal behavior that shocks and upsets the public

bribe money or valuables given to someone to influence behavior, often illegally or unethically

virtue a moral quality

TOPIC 5 — LESSON 6

Lesson Summary

AN UNSETTLED SOCIETY

As the 1920s began, striking differences arose between urban and rural America. Urban Americans enjoyed a rising standard of living and embraced a modern view of the world. City dwellers tended to value education and to be advocates of science and social change.

By contrast, times were hard in rural America. Formal education was considered less important than keeping the farm going. People tended to be conservative about political and social issues, preferring to keep things the way they were. Many rural Americans believed that the Bible was literally true. This belief was called **fundamentalism**. It opposed **modernism**, which stressed science.

The emergence of the Soviet Union as a communist nation compounded the fear of radicals and communists. Communist ideology called for an international workers' revolution, and communist revolts in central and eastern Europe made it seem like the worldwide revolution was starting.

Widespread fear of suspected communists and radicals thought to be plotting revolution within the United States prompted the first American Red Scare. In early 1920, Attorney General A. Mitchell Palmer mounted a series of raids, known as the Palmer Raids. Police arrested thousands of people, some who were radicals and some who were simply immigrants from southern or eastern Europe. To many, these actions seemed to attack the liberties that Americans held most dear.

A wave of immigration inspired nativist politicians to pass laws creating a **quota system** and forcing immigrants to pass a literacy test. The quota system set limits on the number of new immigrants allowed into the United States. Although many Americans appreciated the nation's growing diversity, many did not. In 1915, the Ku Klux Klan was reorganized in Georgia. This violent group, whose leaders had titles such as Grand Dragon and Imperial Wizard, promoted hatred of African Americans, Jews, Catholics, and immigrants.

Another divisive issue of the 1920s was Prohibition. In 1919 the states ratified the Eighteenth Amendment to the United States Constitution, which forbade the manufacture, distribution, and sale (but not consumption) of alcohol. Congress then passed the Volstead Act to enforce the amendment. Police often turned a blind eye to illegal drinking establishments, which left room for **bootleggers** not only to sell alcohol but also to expand into other illegal activities, such as prostitution, drugs, robbery, and murder. Thus, Prohibition unintentionally led to the growth of organized crime.

Lesson Vocabulary

fundamentalism   movement or attitude stressing strict and literal adherence to a set of basic religious principles

modernism   artistic and literary movement sparked by a break with past conventions

quota system   arrangement that limited the number of immigrants who could enter the United States from specific countries

bootlegger   one who sells illegal alcohol

TOPIC 5
LESSON 7

Lesson Summary
THE ROARING TWENTIES

MODIFIED CORNELL NOTES

As urban Americans' wages rose in the 1920s, workers also enjoyed shorter workweeks. For the first time, a large city-dwelling population had free time and money to spend on entertainment. Movies were one of the most popular forms of entertainment and were attended by 60 to 100 million Americans each week. Actors such as comedian Charlie Chaplin, heartthrob Rudolf Valentino, and cowboy William S. Hart became silent film stars. Then, in 1927, the movie The Jazz Singer startled audiences when Al Jolson said, "You ain't seen nothin' yet." The Jazz Singer became the first movie to include sound matched to the action on the screen, and the era of "talkies" was born.

For entertainment at home, Americans bought millions of phonographs and radios. By 1923, almost 600 licensed radio stations broadcast to more than 600,000 radio sets. Americans across the continent listened to the same songs, learned the same dances, and shared a popular culture as never before. People admired the same heroes, such as Babe Ruth, the home-run king, and aviator Charles Lindbergh, who was the first to fly solo across the Atlantic Ocean.

American women challenged political, economic, social, and educational boundaries. With passage of the Nineteenth Amendment, they won the right to vote. Many ran for political office and more joined the workforce. Some women, known as **flappers**, shocked society by wearing short skirts and bobbed hair. At home, new electric appliances made housework easier. Popular magazines, **sociological studies**, novels, and movies all featured the "New Woman" of the 1920s prominently.

A spirit of modernism grew, especially in cities. Austrian psychologist Sigmund Freud contributed to modernism with his theory that human behavior is driven by unconscious desire rather than by rational thought. Painters rejected artistic norms. Writers, including F. Scott Fitzgerald and Ernest Hemingway, wrote about the meaning of life and war. Their literary masterpieces examined **subconscious** desires and the dark side of the American dream.

Lesson Vocabulary

flapper   young woman from the 1920s who defied traditional rules of conduct and dress

sociological study   research into the workings of society, social institutions, and social relationships

subconscious   something that exists in people's minds but is not necessarily known or felt

TOPIC 5 LESSON 8 — Lesson Summary
HARLEM RENAISSANCE

Millions of African Americans left the South after World War I to find racial equity and economic opportunity in the North. In the South, they faced low-paying jobs, substandard schools, Jim Crow oppression, and the threat of lynching. However, they found well-paying jobs, middle-class communities of African American professionals, and a growing political voice in cities such as New York, Chicago, and Detroit.

Harlem in New York City became a **haven** for about 200,000 African Americans from the South as well as black immigrants from the Caribbean. One immigrant was Marcus Garvey, a Jamaican who had traveled widely. After seeing that blacks were treated poorly, Garvey organized a "Back to Africa" movement that urged black unity and separation of the races.

It was F. Scott Fitzgerald who called the 1920s the "Jazz Age." However, it was African Americans who gave the age its **jazz**. A truly **indigenous** American musical form, jazz emerged in the South as a combination of African American and European musical styles. African Americans migrating north brought the new musical style with them. Musicians such as trumpet player Louis Armstrong took jazz to the world. Singer Bessie Smith, nicknamed the "Empress of the Blues," was very popular and became the highest-paid African American entertainer of the 1920s.

The decade also saw the Harlem Renaissance, an outpouring of art and literature that explored the African American experience. Among its most famous writers was Jamaican-born Claude McKay, whose novels and poems were militant calls for action. Langston Hughes celebrated African American culture, and Zora Neale Hurston wrote about women's desire for independence.

The Great Depression ended the Harlem Renaissance. However, the pride and unity it created provided a foundation for the future civil rights movement.

Lesson Vocabulary

haven   a place that offers security and opportunities

jazz   a musical form based on improvisation

indigenous   original or native to a country or region

TOPIC 5	**Review Questions**
	WORLD WAR I AND THE 1920s

Answer the questions below using the information in the Lesson Summaries on the previous pages.

Lesson 1: America Enters World War I

1. Why did the United States get involved in the war?

_____

_____

2. **Identify Causes** Identify the causes of World War I.

_____

_____

Lesson 2: The Home Front During World War I

3. Why did conscientious objectors oppose the war?

_____

_____

4. **Summarize** Summarize how the American government mobilized the public to support the war effort.

_____

_____

Lesson 3 The End of World War I

5. Describe the aims of the Fourteen Points.

_____

_____

6. **Identify Supporting Details** Sequence the events that led the U.S. Senate to not ratify the treaty ending World War I.

_____

_____

Lesson 4: The Postwar Economy Booms

7. How did mass production influence the economy?

_____

_____

8. How did the consumer revolution lead to new ways of purchasing items?

_____

_____

Lesson 5: Government in the 1920s

9. What was the Teapot Dome scandal?

_____

_____

10. **Compare and Contrast** How did the differences between Presidents Harding and Coolidge influence their presidencies?

_____

_____

Lesson 6: An Unsettled Society

11. What did the Eighteenth Amendment forbid?

_____

_____

12. **Contrast** Select an issue that divided Americans. Contrast the ways rural and urban Americans felt about this issue.

_____

_____

Lesson 7: The Roaring Twenties

13. What technological advances led to cultural change during the 1920s?

_____

_____

14. **Summarize** List three ways American culture changed in the 1920s.

_____

_____

Lesson 8: The Harlem Renaissance

15. Why did many African Americans migrate north?

_____

_____

16. **Identify Main Ideas** What was the Harlem Renaissance?

_____

_____

Name _____ Class _____ Date _____

Note Taking Study Guide

THE GREAT DEPRESSION AND THE NEW DEAL

Focus Question: What were the goals of the New Deal and what programs were created to achieve those goals?

As you read, note specific examples of goals and programs and list them in the appropriate column.

The New Deal	
Goals	**Programs**

TOPIC 6 LESSON 1

Lesson Summary
CAUSES OF THE DEPRESSION

The Roaring Twenties were a Republican decade. Beginning in 1920, Republican Presidents led the nation and took credit for the good economic times. In 1928, the country continued to support the Republicans by electing Herbert Hoover as President. However, the nation's prosperity was not as deep or as sturdy as it appeared.

American farmers faced difficult times in the 1920s. They had borrowed money to buy land and machinery to increase the harvest yields during World War I. Although the demand for American crops fell after the war, farmers were still producing large harvests. Cheap food flooded the markets, lowering farmers' profits and making debt repayment hard.

Industrial workers, whose wages rose steadily, did better than farmers. The owners of companies did even better. They became very rich. In fact, in 1929, the wealthiest 0.1 percent of the population earned about the same amount of money (bottom 42 percent combined). However, the people with great wealth could not buy enough goods to keep the economy strong. Still, many workers took advantage of **easy credit** to buy products. This disguised the problem and helped grow the economy.

By 1929, it became clear that too much money was being poured into stock **speculation**. Investors often borrowed money to buy stocks, then sold them to turn a quick profit. Frantic buying and selling inflated the prices of stocks to unrealistic levels. Finally, all the problems began to converge. A sharp drop in stock prices led to panicked selling. Stock prices bottomed out and destroyed whole fortunes in hours on Black Tuesday, October 29, 1929.

The stock market crash marked the beginning of the Great Depression, a period lasting from 1929 to 1941 in which the U.S. economy faltered and unemployment soared. Thousands of banks closed and many businesses failed. The government tried to boost the sale of American goods by passing the Hawley-Smoot Tariff, which placed high taxes on foreign goods. The result was closed markets and unsold goods, which destroyed international trade. Economists still disagree on what was the most important factor leading to the Great Depression, which eventually affected the whole world.

Lesson Vocabulary

easy credit   loan obtained from a lender willing to lend money to a borrower without checking thoroughly that the borrower has the financial ability to repay the loan

speculation   practice of making high-risk investments in hopes of obtaining large profits

TOPIC
6
LESSON 2

Lesson Summary
AMERICANS SUFFER

The Great Depression deeply affected Americans. Some lost everything they had while others struggled simply to survive. In the cities, Americans faced rampant unemployment. Between 1921 and 1929, annual average unemployment rates never rose above 3.7 percent. By 1933, almost 25 percent of workers were without jobs. As unemployed families ran out of money, their hardship deepened. Drastic necessity forced them to sell their belongings. Sometimes a family's only food came from a **bread line**, where people lined up for handouts from charities or public agencies. Many people were evicted from their homes. With no place else to go, they sometimes grouped together in Hoovervilles—makeshift shantytowns of tents and shacks built on public land or vacant lots.

Conditions were bad in rural America, too. Before the depression, farmers had already been struggling. During the depression, their problems worsened. Crop prices dropped lower. Between 1930 and 1934, nearly one million farmers lost their homes for failure to pay their mortgages. Some farmers stayed on the land as **tenant farmers**, working for bigger landowners rather than for themselves. A severe drought and overfarming on the Great Plains turned the soil to dust, making farming impossible and creating huge dust storms. High plains regions in Texas, Oklahoma, Kansas, New Mexico, and Colorado became known as the Dust Bowl. Many farmers left the area and moved to California to look for work. Because some of these people were from Oklahoma, Dust Bowl refugees became known as Okies.

Minorities were hit the hardest by the depression. African American sharecroppers were thrown off the land they had farmed and migrated north. In 1932, unemployment among African Americans was nearly double the national rate. In the Southwest, many white Americans urged **repatriation** of Mexican Americans. Repatriation involved government efforts to send Mexican immigrants and their American children back to Mexico.

For many Americans, the Great Depression was a time of great hopelessness and despair.

Lesson Vocabulary

bread line   line of people waiting for food handouts from charities or public agencies

tenant farmer   farmer who pays rent to a landowner for the use of the land

repatriation   process by which government officials return persons to their country of origin

Lesson Summary

TWO PRESIDENTS RESPOND

MODIFIED CORNELL NOTES

From big cities to small towns, the Great Depression spread misery across America. As the crisis deepened, Herbert Hoover struggled to respond to the nation's problems.

At first, Hoover felt that government should not interfere with what he thought was the natural downswing of the business cycle.

Next, Hoover called for a policy of **localism**. This policy asked state and local government to provide more jobs and relief measures. However, businesses cut wages and laid off workers, towns and states did not have the resources to respond to the crisis, and charities ran low on money.

Finally, the President decided to adopt a policy of **trickle-down economics**. The idea was that the government would provide loans to bankers, and in turn, they could lend money to businesses. Businesses would then hire workers, leading to increased production and consumption as well as the end of the depression. At Hoover's urging, Congress created the Reconstruction Finance Corporation (RFC) to provide loans to businesses. However, businesses did not always use them to hire workers.

Americans became increasingly unhappy with Hoover's handling of the depression. A group of almost 20,000 unemployed World War I veterans known as the Bonus Army marched in protest and set up camps in Washington, D.C. When riots broke out in July 1932, Hoover called in the military.

In November 1932, Franklin D. Roosevelt (FDR) won the presidency by more than 7 million votes.

In his first hundred days in office, FDR proposed and Congress passed 15 bills known as the first New Deal. These measures had three goals: relief, recovery, and reform.

(Continues on the next page.)

Lesson Vocabulary

localism   policy relied on by President Hoover in the early years of the Great Depression, whereby local and state governments act as primary agents of economic relief

trickle-down economics   economic theory that holds that financial benefits given to banks and large businesses will trickle down to smaller businesses and consumers

TOPIC 6
LESSON 3

Lesson Summary
TWO PRESIDENTS RESPOND (continued)

Relief efforts included the establishment of the Tennessee Valley Authority (TVA), which built dams in the Tennessee River valley to control floods and generate electric power, and the creation of the Civilian Conservation Corps (CCC). The CCC provided jobs for more than 2 million young men. They replanted forests, built trails, dug irrigation ditches, and fought fires. Recovery efforts included the National Recovery Administration (NRA) and the Public Works Administration (PWA). The NRA developed industry codes that set **minimum wages** for workers and **minimum prices** for goods. The PWA created millions of new jobs constructing bridges, dams, power plants, and government buildings. Additionally, FDR sought to reform the nation's financial institutions. The Federal Deposit Insurance Corporation (FDIC) insured bank deposits, and the Securities Exchange Commission (SEC) regulated the stock market.

Some Americans thought the New Deal made the government too powerful. Others thought that the New Deal did not provide enough help to citizens. The strongest criticism from this second group came from individuals with roots in the Populist movement.

Lesson Vocabulary

minimum wage   lowest wage allowed by law
minimum price   lowest price allowed by law

Lesson Summary
THE NEW DEAL EXPANDS

President Franklin D. Roosevelt's goals for the first New Deal were relief, recovery, and reform. He used legislation passed by the second New Deal to accomplish the goals of promoting the general welfare and protecting citizens' rights.

In the spring of 1935, Congress created the Works Progress Administration (WPA) to provide new jobs doing public works. The WPA even provided programs to employ displaced artists. The government paid for WPA programs by spending money it didn't have. British economist John Maynard Keynes argued that such **deficit spending** was needed to end the depression.

The Social Security Act created a pension system for retirees, unemployment insurance for workers who lost their jobs, and aid for people with disabilities. New programs aided farmers. The Rural Electrification Administration (REA) helped bring electricity to farms. New laws also aided industrial workers. The Wagner Act gave workers the right to **collective bargaining**. This meant that employers had to negotiate with unions about hours, wages, and other working conditions. The Fair Labor Standards Act of 1938 established a minimum wage and a maximum number of hours for the workweek. It also outlawed child labor.

During the Great Depression there was an upsurge in union activity. The Congress of Industrial Organization (CIO) was established to organize workers in major industries. In 1936, CIO members staged a **sit-down strike** against General Motors, refusing to leave the workplace until a settlement had been reached. Their success led to other strikes, which improved wages and working conditions for union members.

(Continues on the next page.)

Lesson Vocabulary

deficit spending   spending of public funds raised by borrowing

collective bargaining   process in which employers negotiate with labor unions about wages, hours, and other working conditions

sit-down strike   organized labor action in which workers stop working and occupy the workplace until their demands are met

Section Summary
THE NEW DEAL EXPANDS (continued)

FDR faced challenges from the Supreme Court, which struck down a number of the key laws of the New Deal. To dilute the power of the sitting Justices, FDR asked Congress to add six new Justices to the nine-member court, a plan that became known as **court packing**. After 1937, the Supreme Court became more willing to accept New Deal legislation. After a new economic downturn in 1938, FDR chose not to try to force more reforms through Congress.

Lesson Vocabulary

court packing   President Franklin D. Roosevelt's plan to add six new Justices to the nine-member Supreme Court after the Court had ruled some New Deal laws to be unconstitutional

Name _____ Class _____ Date _____

MODIFIED CORNELL NOTES

The New Deal brought fundamental changes to the nation. Some women were provided with the opportunity to increase their political influence. Eleanor Roosevelt transformed the office of First Lady to a politically active position. She traveled extensively and advocated equal justice for all. The first female Cabinet member was Secretary of Labor Frances Perkins, who played a leading role in establishing Social Security and a minimum wage. Despite this, the New Deal did not fight to end gender discrimination in the workplace.

President Roosevelt invited African American leaders to advise him. These unofficial advisers became known as the Black Cabinet. One member, Mary McLeod Bethune, was a powerful champion of racial equality. Even so, racial discrimination and injustice continued to plague African Americans.

The Indian New Deal was a program to help American Indians by providing funding for the construction of new schools and hospitals. In 1934, the Indian Reorganization Act restored tribal control of American Indian lands. The Bureau of Indian Affairs also stopped discouraging the practice of traditional American Indian customs.

By his death in 1945, FDR had united a culturally diverse group of Americans into a strong political force called the New Deal coalition, which gave the Democratic Party a sizable majority in both houses of Congress. FDR and the New Deal also helped to unify the nation. Programs such as the WPA allowed people of varied backgrounds to get to know one another, breaking down regional and ethnic prejudices.

New Deal programs increased the size and scope of the federal government like never before. The government assumed responsibility for providing for the welfare of children as well as the poor, elderly, sick, disabled, and unemployed. This led to the rise of a **welfare state**.

The expanding role of the government, including the creation of many new federal agencies, gave the executive branch much more power. Roosevelt was elected President four times. After his death, there was a call for limiting the President's term of office. In 1951, the Twenty-second Amendment limited the President to two consecutive terms in office.

Lesson Vocabulary

welfare state   government that assumes responsibility for providing for the welfare of the poor, elderly, sick, and unemployed

TOPIC 6 LESSON 6

Lesson Summary

CULTURE DURING THE DEPRESSION

Entertainment became big business during the 1930s, creating a golden age in American culture. Large radio networks dominated the airwaves, while a cluster of film companies ruled the silver screen. Radio ownership grew during the decade, and nearly two thirds of all Americans attended at least one movie a week.

The movies were a form of escapism during the Great Depression as Americans sought relief from their concerns. Movies like The Wizard of Oz promised weary audiences that their dreams really could come true. In the early 1930s, many films reflected the public's distrust of **big business** and government. Others, such as the films of Frank Capra, celebrated American idealism and the triumph of the common man over adversity.

Radio brought news and entertainment into American homes. FDR used fireside radio chats to explain his New Deal programs. National radio networks broadcasted dramas, comedies, soap operas, and variety shows. Episodes from *The Lone Ranger* began running in 1933 and lasted for more than 20 years. Sometimes the lines between news and entertainment were blurred. When the Mercury Theatre broadcasted a drama called *War of the Worlds* on October 30, 1938, many people panicked, believing that Martians were actually invading.

Music also provided a diversion from hard times, whether on the radio at home or in nightclubs. Americans enjoyed "swing" music played by "big bands." Blues singers focused on the harsh conditions faced by African Americans. Woody Guthrie wrote ballads about the Okies, farmers who fled the Dust Bowl.

The federal government funded the arts for the first time through programs such as the Federal Art Project. Artists painted huge **murals** on public buildings across the nation. Dorothea Lange and other photographers documented the plight of American farmers.

Many writers produced novels featuring working-class heroes. John Steinbeck's *The Grapes of Wrath* traces the fictional Joad family from the Oklahoma Dust Bowl to California. Lillian Hellman wrote several plays featuring strong roles for women as well as screenplays for movies. Americans also enjoyed comic strips and comic books.

Lesson Vocabulary

big business large-scale businesses controlled by corporations

murals large painting applied directly to a wall or a ceiling

TOPIC 6 — Review Questions
THE GREAT DEPRESSION AND THE NEW DEAL

Answer the questions below using the information in the Lesson Summaries on the previous pages.

Lesson 1: Causes of the Depression

1. In 1928, how did Americans show their approval for the way Republicans handled the economy?

_____

_____

2. **Cause and Effect** Select a cause of the Great Depression. Explain how it contributed to the depression.

_____

_____

_____

Lesson 2: Americans Suffer

3. What was repatriation, and who was most affected by it?

_____

_____

_____

4. **Categorize** What were some of the problems present in both urban and rural America?

_____

_____

_____

Lesson 3 Two Presidents Respond

5. Name two New Deal policies that provided immediate relief to Americans.

_____

_____

6. **Identify Supporting Details** List the details that support the conclusion that Hoover's policy of volunteerism failed.

_____

_____

_____

Lesson 4: The New Deal Expands

7. Explain how New Deal legislation promoted the well-being of workers.

_____

_____

_____

8. **Connect Ideas** How did the policies of the second New Deal improve the standard of living of Americans?

_____

_____

Lesson 5: Effects of the New Deal

9. How did the New Deal lead to the rise of a welfare state?

_____

_____

10. **Identify Main Ideas** How did the New Deal benefit different groups in American society?

_____

_____

Lesson 6 Culture During the Depression

11. **Identify Main Ideas and Details** In what ways were the 1930s a golden age for entertainment?

_____

_____

12. What was the Federal Art Project?

_____

_____

Focus Question: In what ways did Americans contribute to their nation's war effort during World War II, and how did these contributions create new opportunities for certain groups of people in America who participated in the war?

As you read, note specific examples of contributions that different groups of people made. Write these in the empty spaces of the web that surround the central core labeled "Contributions."

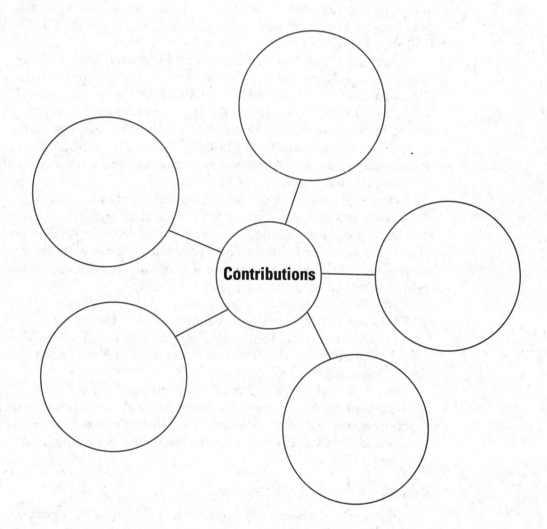

Contributions

TOPIC 7 LESSON 1

Lesson Summary
RISE OF AGGRESSIVE DICTATORS

In the 1920s, some nations moved toward democracy. Others moved toward repressive dictatorships and **totalitarianism**, a type of government in which a single party or leader controls the economic, social, and cultural lives of a nation's people.

The 1917 communist revolution in the Soviet Union produced the first totalitarian state, headed by Vladimir Lenin. In 1924, Joseph Stalin took his place as the Communist Party's head.

A postwar economic depression troubled Italy. In 1922, the king asked the founder of the Fascist Party, Benito Mussolini, to form a government. Mussolini turned Italy into a fascist country with a controlled press, secret police, and no political parties.

Following World War I, Germany became a democracy. However, the Great Depression caused severe economic troubles in the 1930s. The National Socialist German Workers' Party (Nazi Party) led by Adolf Hitler rose to power. Hitler criticized many people, political programs, and ideologies, but his sharpest assaults were against communists and Jews. Hitler was violently **anti-Semitic**, or prejudiced against Jewish people. He was appointed to chancellor in 1933 and became president of Germany within two years.

In Japan, the Great Depression ended a period of increased democracy and peaceful change. Military leaders argued that expansion throughout Asia would solve Japan's problems. Japan attacked Manchuria and established a puppet state in 1931. Six years later, Japan attacked China again, raiding the capital city with such brutality that it became known as the "Rape of Nanjing."

In the 1930s, Italy and Germany resorted to acts of aggression similar to those of Japan in Asia. Hitler reclaimed the Saar region from French control and sent troops into the Rhineland, while Mussolini led an invasion into Ethiopia. The League of Nations did almost nothing to stop aggression.

France, Britain, and the United States pursued the policy of **appeasement** toward the fascist leaders. Appeasement means granting concessions to a potential enemy to maintain peace. However, this approach only encouraged the leaders to become bolder and more aggressive.

Lesson Vocabulary

totalitarianism   a theory of government in which a single party or leader controls the economic, social, and cultural lives of its people

anti-Semitic   prejudiced against Jewish people

appeasement   policy of granting concessions in order to keep peace

TOPIC 7 — LESSON 2 — Lesson Summary
AMERICA DEBATES INVOLVEMENT

After Japan's violent attack on China in 1937, President Roosevelt criticized the Japanese aggression. The United States, however, continued to back away from intervention in foreign conflicts.

Despite a military alliance among France, Britain, and Poland, Germany invaded Poland in 1939. Britain and France declared war on Germany, and World War II had begun. The Axis Powers would come to include Germany, Italy, Japan, and several other nations. The Axis Powers fought the Allies, which included Britain, France, and eventually the Soviet Union, China, and the United States.

Germany used a new technique called **blitzkrieg**, or "lightning war." Tanks and planes attacked in a coordinated effort and quickly conquered Poland. In April 1940, Denmark and Norway fell to the German blitzkrieg. In May, Germany took the Netherlands, Belgium, and Luxembourg, and then invaded France. The next month, Germany attacked Britain from the air.

Winston Churchill, the prime minister of Britain, hoped to convince the United States to join the Allies. Accounts by news reporter Edward R. Murrow on the bombing of London shocked the American public. Murrow emphasized that the Germans were bombing civilians, not armies or military sites. Despite its isolationist policies, the United States moved slowly toward involvement. Congress passed the Neutrality Act of 1939. This law helped the Allies buy goods and munitions from the United States. Isolationists, however, believed that getting involved in a bloody European war would be wasteful and dangerous.

Even though most Americans wanted to remain **neutral**, President Roosevelt constantly argued for helping Britain. In early 1941, Congress approved the Lend-Lease Act. This act gave the President the power to sell, give, or lease weapons to protect the United States. In 1941, Roosevelt also met with Churchill to discuss the war. They signed the Atlantic Charter, a document that endorsed national self-determination and an international system of "general security." The agreement signaled the deepening alliance between the two nations. Hitler was not blind to American support of the Allies. In the fall of 1941, he ordered German U-boats to attack American ships. U.S. involvement in the war seemed inevitable.

Lesson Vocabulary

blitzkrieg "lightning war" that emphasized the use of speed and firepower to penetrate deep into the enemy's territory

neutral not supporting any side in a war

MODIFIED CORNELL NOTES

TOPIC 7 — LESSON 3

Lesson Summary

AMERICA ENTERS WORLD WAR II

As Japan expanded its empire throughout Asia, its relationship with the United States worsened. Japan needed resources such as oil, steel, and rubber to maintain its military. The United States began to withhold these goods to limit Japan's expansion. The United States also instituted a **trade embargo** against Japan.

At first, Hideki Tojo, the Japanese prime minister, tried to keep the United States neutral. However, when a trade agreement with the United States failed, Tojo decided on a decisive military strike. On December 7, 1941, hundreds of Japanese airplanes bombed the site of the United States Navy's main base in the Pacific at Pearl Harbor, Hawaii. Nearly 2,500 people were killed in this devastating surprise attack. Many ships were sunk, and hundreds of aircraft were destroyed or damaged.

Congress immediately declared war on Japan. Germany and Italy then declared war on the United States. George Marshall, United States Army chief of staff, triggered plans for building up the military as quickly as possible. Meanwhile, men from all ethnic and racial backgrounds joined branches of the military by the millions. Thousands of women joined the Women's Army Corps (WAC) as clerical workers, truck drivers, instructors, and lab technicians. The government also created agencies to ensure the production of supplies needed for the military. These agencies allocated scarce materials to the proper industries. Private companies developed innovative production techniques to make huge quantities of war goods, creating a production miracle that was key to helping the Allies fight the war.

In Asia, United States Army General Douglas MacArthur struggled unsuccessfully to hold the Philippines against the Japanese forces. U.S. forces had to retreat, and MacArthur evacuated to Australia in March. Some 70,000 U.S. and Filipino troops fell back to the Bataan Peninsula and the citadel on Corregidor Island, where they lived on half and quarter rations. In April 1942, the soldiers on the Bataan Peninsula surrendered. Japanese troops forced these sick and malnourished men to march many miles. More than 7,000 American and Filipino troops died on the march, which is known as the Bataan Death March. Finally, in May 1942, the **citadel** on Corregidor Island surrendered, leaving Japan in control of the Philippines.

By the summer of 1942, Japan controlled most of Southeast Asia and the western Pacific. Then in May 1942, the United States Navy finally began to stop the Japanese advance. At the Battle of Coral Sea, the United States Navy prevented Japan from taking a key spot in New Guinea. The Japanese offensive was over.

Lesson Vocabulary

trade embargo   prohibition of trade with a particular country

citadel   fortress

TOPIC 7 LESSON 4

Lesson Summary
A WAR ON TWO FRONTS

The attack on Pearl Harbor brought the United States into World War II. The Allies' ultimate goal was to fight and win a two-front war. Their first objective, however, was to defeat Hitler. The United States was producing millions of tons of guns, tanks, and other supplies. German U-boats, however, had sunk over 3,500 merchant ships bound for Britain. By mid-1943, using radar, bombers, and underwater depth charges, Allied forces were sinking U-boats faster than Germany could manufacture them. The Allies had begun to win the war in the North Atlantic.

In 1941, Germany attacked Russia, and Stalin wanted Roosevelt and Churchill to open a second front in France. In early 1942, British planes instead began **saturation bombing**, dropping large numbers of bombs on German cities. American bombers used **strategic bombing**, targeting key political and industrial centers. The Tuskegee Airmen, an African American fighter squadron, played a key role in the bombing campaign. In January 1943, after the long, bitter Battle of Stalingrad, the Russians turned back the German invasion of their country. During the same month, FDR announced that only the **unconditional surrender** of the Axis Powers would end the war. That is, they had to give up completely.

To help pave the way for an invasion of Italy, the Allies decided to push the Germans out of North Africa, where they had been fighting British troops since 1940. In February 1942, American General Dwight Eisenhower commanded the Allied invasion. After difficult battles, General George S. Patton, Jr. took charge of American forces. In May 1943, German and Italian forces in North Africa surrendered. Two months later, Allied forces invaded Sicily, two miles off the mainland of Italy. From there, they launched their invasion of Italy, and in September, Italy surrendered.

In spite of its "Europe first" strategy, the United States did not ignore the Pacific where Japanese forces had continued to advance. In June 1942, the Japanese attacked Midway, a vital American naval base in the central Pacific. The American naval commander, Admiral Chester Nimitz, had learned of the Japanese plans, and the Battle of Midway was a decisive American victory. It ended Japanese expansion in the Pacific and put Japan on the defensive.

Lesson Vocabulary

saturation bombing   tactic of dropping massive amounts of bombs in order to inflict maximum damage

strategic bombing   tactic of dropping bombs on key political and industrial targets

unconditional surrender   giving up completely without any concessions

Name _____ Class _____ Date _____

MODIFIED CORNELL NOTES

World War II fears and tensions tested civil liberties, but the war also provided new opportunities for women and minorities. Many women found jobs, especially in heavy industry. They gained confidence, knowledge, organizational experience, and a paycheck. However, few African Americans found meaningful employment with defense employers. In response, African American labor leader A. Philip Randolph planned a massive march on Washington, D.C., to protest employment discrimination. Under pressure, FDR issued Executive Order 8802. It assured fair hiring practices in any job funded with government money.

Wartime needs encouraged people to move to the South and Southwest to find jobs in defense industries. To alleviate the rural population drain, the United States initiated the *bracero* program. This program brought Mexican laborers to work on farms in the United States. Although they often faced discrimination, braceros contributed greatly to the war effort.

After the attack on Pearl Harbor, the federal government moved about 100,000 Japanese Americans living on the West Coast to camps in isolated locations under a policy of **internment**. There, they were held in jail-like conditions for the duration of the war. Some Japanese Americans went to court to seek their rights. In the 1944 case of *Korematsu* v. *United States*, the Supreme Court upheld the government's wartime internment policy. When the government lifted a ban on Japanese Americans serving in the armed forces, many enlisted. The Japanese American 442nd Regimental Combat Team fought in the Italian campaign and became the most decorated military unit in American history.

The war cost the United States $330 billion. To help pay for it, Congress levied a tax on all working Americans. **Rationing** was instituted to ensure that there would be adequate raw materials, such as oil and rubber, for war production. The federal Office of War Information (OWI) worked with the media to encourage support of the war effort. Millions of Americans bought war bonds and contributed to the war effort in many other ways, large and small.

Lesson Vocabulary

internment   temporary imprisonment of members of a specific group

rationing   government-controlled limits on the amount of certain goods that civilians could buy during wartime

TOPIC 7 LESSON 6 — Lesson Summary
THE ALLIES WIN WORLD WAR II

In 1943, the Allied leaders agreed to open a second front in France. On June 6, 1944, known as D-Day, British and American forces traveled across the English Channel to invade France from the west. More than 11,000 planes prepared the way, followed by more than 4,400 ships and landing crafts. By the end of the day, they had gained a toehold in France. On July 1, more than one million Allied troops had landed.

Germany now faced a hopeless two-front war because the Soviets were advancing from the east. In December 1944, Hitler ordered a counterattack, known as the Battle of the Bulge. Hitler's scenario called for German forces to capture communication and transportation hubs. The attack almost succeeded. However, with help from their bombers, the Allies managed to push the Germans out of France. By January 1945, the Soviet Army had reached the Oder River outside Berlin, and in April, the United States Army was just 50 miles west of Berlin. Hitler committed suicide on April 30, and on May 7, Germany surrendered.

American forces in the Pacific followed an **island-hopping** strategy in a steady path toward Japan. Japanese troops fought hard, and Japanese **kamikaze** pilots deliberately crashed their planes into American ships. By April 1945, American pilots finally made their way to Okinawa, 340 miles from Japan. From Okinawa, American pilots could bomb the Japanese home islands. American bombers hit factories, military bases, and cities.

Advances in technology helped determine the final outcome of the war. Albert Einstein, a famous scientist, had alerted FDR of the need to proceed with atomic development. Physicist J. Robert Oppenheimer was in charge of the scientific aspect of the program, known as the Manhattan Project. On the morning of July 16, 1945, the first atomic bomb was tested. In order to save American lives and to end the war, President Harry S. Truman decided to use the atomic bomb against Japan. On August 6, 1945, U.S. pilots dropped at atomic bomb on Hiroshima. Three days later, the United States dropped a second atomic bomb on Nagasaki. Emperor Hirohito made the decision to surrender, and on August 15, the Allies celebrated V-J (Victory in Japan) Day. World War II had been the most costly war in history. As many as 60 million people—mostly civilians—had died in the conflict.

Lesson Vocabulary

island-hopping   World War II strategy that involved seizing selected Japanese-held islands in the Pacific while bypassing others

kamikaze   Japanese pilots who deliberately crashed planes into American ships during World War II

TOPIC 7

LESSON 7

Lesson Summary
THE HOLOCAUST

In 1945, there was no word for the Holocaust, the most horrific event of World War II. It was the Nazi attempt to kill all Jews, as well as other "undesirables," under their control. This was part of a racist Nazi ideology that considered Aryans—white northern European gentiles—superior to other people.

Hitler began to persecute the Jews as soon as he came to power. In 1935, the Nuremberg Laws denied citizenship to Jews and segregated them at every level of society. Acts of violence against Jews were common. The most serious occurred on November 9, 1938, and is called Kristallnacht, the "Night of Broken Glass." Secret police and military units destroyed more than 200 synagogues and 7,500 Jewish businesses, killed more than 200 Jews, and injured more than 600 others.

Hitler's "Final Solution to the Jewish question" was **genocide**, the willful annihilation of all Jews living in regions under his control. Jews and other "undesirables" were confined in **concentration camps**. In theory, the camps were designed to turn prisoners into "useful members" of the Third Reich. However, there were no restraints on guards, who tortured and killed prisoners without fear of reprisals. Doctors conducted experiments that killed prisoners or left them deformed. Many concentration camps were **death camps**, where prisoners were systematically exterminated. The largest death camp was Auschwitz in southern Poland.

Before the war, the United States and other countries could have done more if they had relaxed immigration policies and accepted more Jewish refugees. Once the war started, news of the mass killings began to filter to the West. In early 1944, FDR began to respond and established the War Refugee Board, which worked with the Red Cross to save thousands of Eastern European Jews. The enormity of the Nazi crime became real for most Americans only when Allied soldiers began to liberate the concentration camps. The revelation of the Holocaust increased American support for a Jewish homeland. Therefore, when Jewish settlers in Palestine proclaimed the state of Israel, President Truman immediately recognized the new nation.

Lesson Vocabulary

genocide willful annihilation of a racial, political, or cultural group

concentration camps camps used by the Nazis to imprison "undesirable" members of society

death camps Nazi camps designed for the extermination of prisoners

TOPIC 7 — LESSON 8

Lesson Summary
IMPACT OF WORLD WAR II

As World War II drew to an end, Japan and Germany kept fighting long after their defeat was certain. The protracted fighting gave the Allies time to make plans for a postwar world. In February 1945, Roosevelt, Churchill, and Stalin met at Yalta on the Black Sea. At the Yalta Conference, they discussed final strategy and crucial questions concerning postwar Germany, Eastern Europe, and Asia. A few months later, the Big Three, now composed of Stalin, Truman, and Attlee, met at Potsdam to formalize the decision to divide Germany into four zones of occupation. The war ended Western European domination of the world. Two **superpowers**—the United States and the Soviet Union—became the predominant nations of the postwar world.

Not all the changes that took place after the war ended were what the Allies had envisioned at Yalta and Potsdam. Communist and anticommunist interests clashed in Eastern Europe. Civil war resumed in China. Under American military occupation, Japan gained a new constitution that abolished the armed forces and enacted democratic reforms.

The United States, where industry had boomed during the war, helped to shape the postwar world economy. The United States also led the charge to establish the United Nations (UN). While it was organized on the basis of the Great Powers, all member nations sat on the General Assembly. In 1948, the UN issued the Universal Declaration of Human Rights, which condemns slavery and torture, upholds freedom of speech and religion, and affirms the right to an adequate standard of living.

During the war, the Axis Powers had repeatedly violated the Geneva Convention, which governs the humane treatment of wounded soldiers and prisoners of war. More than a thousand Japanese were tried for war crimes, and at the Nuremberg Trials, key leaders of Nazi Germany were brought to justice for their crimes against humanity.

Americans had closely followed the war and learned to think in global terms. They defined themselves as democratic, tolerant, and peaceful. The war gave renewed vigor to the fight for civil rights at home. It also ushered in a period of economic growth and prosperity.

Lesson Vocabulary

superpowers   strong nations that dominated the postwar world

TOPIC 7	**Review Questions**
	WORLD WAR II

Answer the questions below using the information in the Lesson Summaries on the previous pages.

Lesson 1: Rise of Aggressive Dictators

1. Summarize Name the countries and leaders discussed in this section.

_____

_____

2. How did the military leaders of Japan want to solve the country's problems?

_____

_____

Lesson 2: America Debates Involvement

3. What was President Roosevelt's position on the war in Europe?

_____

_____

4. Sequence List the countries Germany conquered by order of date.

_____

_____

Lesson 3: America Enters World War II

5. Identify Causes and Effects What was the United States' immediate reaction to the attack on Pearl Harbor?

_____

_____

6. Why was the Battle of Coral Sea so important to the United States?

_____

_____

Lesson 4: A War on Two Fronts

7. Why was it so important for the United States to defeat the Japanese at Midway?

_____

_____

8. Summarize How did the Allies prepare for the invasion of Italy?

_____

_____

TOPIC 7

Review Questions

WORLD WAR II (continued)

Lesson 5: The Home Front

9. What was the bracero program?

_____

_____

10. Identify Main Ideas How did the workplace change as a result of World War II?

_____

_____

Lesson 6: The Allies Win World War II

11. What was involved in the D-Day invasion of France?

_____

_____

12. Recognize Sequence Number the following events in chronological order.

Japan surrenders.

The first atomic bomb is tested.

Germany surrenders.

_____

_____

Lesson 7: The Holocaust

13. What was the purpose of Hitler's concentration camps?

_____

_____

14. Recognize Sequence What happened to Jews in Germany after Hitler came to power?

_____

_____

Lesson 8: Impact of World War II

15. What long-term changes were brought about by World War II?

_____

_____

16. Understand Effects Which effect of World War II would help to prevent future wars?

_____

_____

Name _____ Class _____ Date _____

Focus Question: How did the United States and its Allies resist the spread of communism throughout the world? How was this done both politically and socially?

As you read, note specific examples of how the United States resisted communism through international actions as well as through domestic changes.

Resistance to Communism	
International Actions	**Domestic Changes**
1.	1.
2.	2.
3.	3.
4.	4.
5.	5.
6.	6.
7.	7.
8.	8.

TOPIC 8 LESSON 1
Lesson Summary
THE BEGINNING OF THE COLD WAR

When Roosevelt, Stalin, and Churchill met at Yalta in February 1945, it was clear that the Allies would defeat Germany. The United States and Great Britain wanted a united Germany and independent nations in Eastern Europe after the war. Soviet dictator Stalin wanted a weak, divided Germany and an Eastern Europe under communist control. Despite Stalin's promises, Poland, Czechoslovakia, Hungary, Romania, and Bulgaria became **satellite states** of the Soviet Union, along with the eastern part of Germany. After another meeting that summer at Potsdam, Harry S. Truman, who was now President, became convinced that the Soviet Union had aspirations toward world domination. Thus began the 46-year long Cold War.

Churchill agreed with President Truman and said an **iron curtain** had descended upon Europe. East of the curtain, Stalin was tightening his grip and trying to spread communism to other countries. Truman asked Congress for money to help Turkey and Greece fight communism. His promise of aid became known as the Truman Doctrine. It set a new course for American foreign policy.

The goal of another American policy, called **containment**, was to use American power to help nations resist communism. Containment's first success was based on Secretary of State George C. Marshall's economic recovery plan for Europe. Under the Marshall Plan, which began in 1948, the United States gave about $13 billion in grants and loans to Western European nations.

In June 1948, Stalin decided to block all shipping from western Germany into West Berlin—deep inside communist East Germany—hoping that would make the city fall to the communists. The United States and Britain stopped his plan by airlifting supplies, including food, fuel, and clothing, into West Berlin.

The Berlin Airlift showed that communism could be contained. To continue to block Soviet expansion, the North Atlantic Treaty Organization (NATO), formed in 1949. Twelve Western European and North American nations agreed to act together to defend Western Europe. In 1955, West Germany joined NATO. In response, the Soviet Union and its satellite states formed the Warsaw Pact. All communist states of Eastern Europe except Yugoslavia promised to defend one another if attacked.

Lesson Vocabulary

satellite states   independent nations under the control of a more powerful nation

iron curtain   term coined by Winston Churchill to describe the border between the Soviet satellite states and Western Europe

containment   policy of keeping communism contained within its existing borders

TOPIC 8 LESSON 2

Lesson Summary

THE KOREAN WAR

MODIFIED CORNELL NOTES

Since the Russian Revolution, the Soviets had tried to export communism around the world, sure that it would reach worldwide influence. Events in China in 1949 seemed to prove them right.

Chinese nationalist leader Jiang Jieshi (known as Chiang Kaishek in the United States) and communist leader Mao Zedong had been allies against Japan during World War II, but once the war ended, they became enemies. The United States supported Jiang, while the Soviet Union aided Mao. In 1949, Mao's communists took over the Chinese mainland, calling their government the People's Republic of China.

From there, the conflict over communism moved to Korea. After World War II, the United States and the Soviet Union had split Korea into two nations divided by the 38th parallel of latitude. On June 25, 1950, about 90,000 North Korean troops armed with Soviet weapons crossed the 38th parallel to attack South Korea.

President Truman sent American troops to join South Korean and United Nations forces. Under a World War II hero, General Douglas MacArthur, they attacked the port city of Inchon in September 1950. By October, they drove the North Koreans back north.

Truman worried what China might do if the war continued, but MacArthur told him China would not intervene and he continued to push northward. Then, on November 26, 1950, around 300,000 Chinese soldiers attacked. Truman did not want the United States to enter into a major war that would involve huge numbers of troops and maybe even atomic weapons, but MacArthur distrusted Truman's policy of a "**limited war**." When MacArthur sent a letter to Congress condemning the policy, Truman fired him.

By the spring of 1951, the war settled into a stalemate. To achieve a cease-fire in 1953, Dwight D. Eisenhower, now President, hinted he might use nuclear weapons.

No side won the Korean War, and the two Koreas remain divided today. But two things did change: Truman's use of American forces enlarged the power of the presidency, and a new alliance called the Southeast Asia Treaty Organization (SEATO) was formed to prevent the spread of communism. It was the Asian version of NATO.

Lesson Vocabulary

limited war   worldwide rivalry between the United States and the Soviet Union

TOPIC 8 LESSON 3

Lesson Summary
THE COLD WAR INTENSIFIES

On September 2, 1949, Americans learned that the Soviets now had an atomic bomb. The following month, communists took over China. For Americans, the world had suddenly become more threatening.

Truman soon ordered the development of a hydrogen bomb. Some scientists warned that developing the H-Bomb would lead to a perpetual **arms race**. For the next four decades, the United States and the Soviet Union stockpiled nuclear weapons. Each hoped this program of **mutually assured destruction** would prevent the other from actually using the weapons.

President Dwight D. Eisenhower continued to stockpile nuclear weapons. His foreign policy emphasized **massive retaliation**. Eisenhower's Secretary of State, John Foster Dulles, believed that only by going to the brink of war—an approach called **brinksmanship**—could the United States discourage communist aggression.

Nikita Khrushchev, who became leader of the Soviet Union in 1953, continued to try to spread communism. In 1956, workers in Poland rioted against Soviet rule and won greater control of their government. But when students and workers in Hungary tried a similar thing, Khrushchev crushed the revolt.

In the Middle East, Egyptian President Gamal Abdel Nasser wanted to build a dam on the Nile River. When he opened relations with communist China and the Soviet Union, the United States withdrew its offer to help. Nasser then **nationalized** the Suez Canal. In response, Britain, France, and Israel invaded Egypt in October 1956. Using the Suez crisis as an excuse, Britain and France took control of the canal but withdrew when Eisenhower would not support them.

Eisenhower then announced the United States would use force to help any nation threatened by communism. The Eisenhower Doctrine was used in 1958 to put down a revolt against a pro-American government in Lebanon. The Eisenhower administration also used the Central Intelligence Agency (CIA) to help return pro-American governments to Iran and Guatemala.

Lesson Vocabulary

arms race   competition between superpowers to build more powerful nuclear weapons

mutually assured destruction   policy in which the United States and the Soviet Union hoped to deter nuclear war by building up enough weapons to destroy one another

massive retaliation   policy of threatening to use massive force in response to aggression

brinksmanship   belief that only by going to the brink of war could the United States protect itself against Soviet aggression

nationalized   to place a private resource under government control

MODIFIED CORNELL NOTES

TOPIC 8 LESSON 4

Lesson Summary
COLD WAR FEARS AT HOME

In 1947, the Red Scare—public fear that communists were working to destroy America both from within and without the country—spurred President Truman to investigate federal employees. About 3,000 people were dismissed or resigned. The Truman administration also used the 1940 Smith Act, a law against advocating violent overthrow of the government, to send 11 U.S. Communist Party members to prison.

Meanwhile, the House Committee on Un-American Activities (HUAC) investigated **subversive** activities throughout American life, including academic institutions, labor unions, and city halls. In 1947, HUAC targeted the Hollywood Ten, a group of left-wing writers, directors, and producers. They refused to testify against themselves but were sent to prison. Movie executives then circulated a **blacklist** that named entertainment figures suspected of communist ties, shattering many careers.

Two sensational spy trials increased the country's suspicion of communists. The first one concerned Alger Hiss, a government employee who had helped organize the United Nations. In 1948, Whittaker Chambers, a former member of the Communist Party and an espionage agent, named Hiss as one of his government contacts. Hiss denied everything before HUAC but was sentenced to five years in prison. The second trial involved Julius and Ethel Rosenberg, who were accused of passing secret information about nuclear science to Soviet agents. The Rosenbergs claimed that they were being persecuted because they were Jewish and held unpopular beliefs. They were convicted in a highly controversial trial and executed in 1953.

Joseph R. McCarthy, a senator from Wisconsin, also increased Americans' fears. He claimed he had a long list of communists in the State Department, but each time he was asked to give specific names and numbers, his figures changed. Still, with the outbreak of the Korean War in 1950, McCarthy's popularity soared. McCarthyism became a catchword for the senator's vicious style of reckless charges. McCarthy's targets grew bigger, and in 1954, he went after the United States Army. After viewers saw him badger witnesses and twist the truth during televised hearings, he lost his strongest supporters. The end of the Korean War in 1953 and McCarthy's downfall in 1954 signaled the decline of the Red Scare.

Lesson Vocabulary

subversive describing a secretive act done with the intention of overthrowing or destroying a government or political system

blacklist list of persons who were not hired because of suspected communist ties

TOPIC 8 LESSON 5

Lesson Summary

POSTWAR PROSPERITY

The production of military supplies halted at the end of World War II. Millions of Americans initially lost their jobs, but soon the nation experienced the longest period of economic growth in American history.

President Harry Truman brought soldiers home by starting the **demobilization**, or the process of sending home members of the army. To calm fears about the economy, the government passed the law known as the GI Bill of Rights. The GI Bill provided veterans with unemployment benefits, financial aid for college, and loans to start businesses.

Many veterans started families upon returning home. This **baby boom** peaked in 1957 when 4.3 million babies were born. Between 1940 and 1955, the U.S. population grew by 27 percent. Soaring demand for consumer products caused skyrocketing prices and inflation.

Southern and western states, known as the Sunbelt, also experienced rapid growth. These states had appealing climates and a large number of jobs in the defense, aerospace, and electronics industries. As people moved, their political power moved with them. The Sunbelt and suburbs gained representation while urban areas in the Northeast and the Midwest lost political power.

The U.S. economy was also shifting. Fewer people worked in manufacturing or farming. Employment grew in the **service sector**, businesses that provided services rather than manufactured goods, and **information industries**, businesses that provided informational services. **Franchise businesses** allowed companies to distribute their products and services through retail outlets owned by independent operators. **Multinational corporations**, companies that produced and sold their goods and services across the globe, thrived.

(Continues on the next page.)

Lesson Vocabulary

demobilization   sending home members of the army

baby boom   increase in births between 1945 and 1964

service sector   businesses that provide services rather than manufactured goods

information industries   businesses that provide informational services

franchise businesses   to allow companies to distrubute their products or services through retail outlets owned by independent operators

multinational corporations   companies that produce and sell their goods and services all over the world

TOPIC
8
LESSON 5

Lesson Summary

POSTWAR PROSPERITY (continued)

Unions also experienced change. The AFL and the CIO joined in 1955 to form the AFL-CIO, bringing them more political clout. However, new white-collar workers generally did not join unions.

The inflation rate prompted several trade unions to demand pay increases. When employers refused, millions of workers went on strike. Congress then enacted the Taft-Hartley Act to outlaw the closed shop—a workplace that hired only union members.

After the election, Truman introduced the Fair Deal, a program that would strengthen New Deal reforms and establish programs such as national health insurance. Most of the Fair Deal failed in Congress.

In 1952, Republican Dwight Eisenhower won the presidency by a landslide. He helped create an interstate highway system and gave financial support to education.

TOPIC 8 — LESSON 6
Lesson Summary
MASS CULTURE IN THE 1950s

Between 1940 and 1960, more than 40 million Americans moved to the suburbs, one of the largest mass migrations in history. Developers quickly began building affordable housing in the suburbs to fill the gap left by a shortage of urban housing. Government-backed low-interest loans enabled more people to purchase homes.

Suburban growth would not have been possible had Congress not passed the Interstate Highway Act in 1956. This act authorized funds to build 41,000 miles of highway, consisting of multilane expressways that would connect the nation's major cities. The new highways eased the commute from suburbs to cities and boosted the travel and vacation industries.

As the U.S. economy began to boom in the postwar era, Americans were caught up in a wave of **consumerism**, buying as much as they could, much of it on credit. **Median family income** refers to average family income. Median family income rose dramatically during the 1950s. With money to spend, easy credit, and new goods to buy, shopping became a new pastime for Americans.

During the 1950s, the ideal family was one in which men worked and women stayed home. Popular magazines of the era described the **nuclear family**, or a household consisting of a mother and father and their children, as the backbone of American society. Nevertheless, as the 1950s progressed, more women were willing to challenge the view that a woman should not have a career.

More so than in the past, family life revolved around children. Dr. Benjamin Spock, a best-selling author of the era, emphasized the importance of nurturing children, from their earliest days as infants through their teen years.

Television had a profound impact on American society, particularly among children. Sitcoms, which rarely discussed real-life problems, were popular. These shows reflected and reinforced the ideal of the 1950s family. Television also eroded distinct regional and ethnic cultures, helping to develop a national culture.

Educational opportunities grew as well. By the early 1960s, almost 40 percent of college-age Americans attended college, up from about 15 percent in 1940. The federal government increased education funds, in part to produce more scientists and science teachers. Many states improved their public universities. Ordinary Americans' access to higher education also increased. California created a California Master Plan, creating three tiers of higher education: research universities, state colleges, and community colleges.

Lesson Vocabulary

consumerism   large-scale buying, much of it on credit

median family income   a measure of average family income

nuclear family   an ideal or typical household with a father, mother, and children

MODIFIED CORNELL NOTES

TOPIC 8
LESSON 7

Lesson Summary

SOCIAL ISSUES OF THE 1950s

Despite the prosperity of the 1950s, not everyone benefited from it. Some Americans were dissatisfied with the changes brought by affluence. Social critics and a small group of writers and artists known as **beatniks** criticized what they viewed as the crass materialism and conformity of the American middle class. The theme of alienation, or the feeling of being cut off from mainstream society, dominated many of the era's popular novels.

Like television, **rock-and-roll** captured the attention of Americans. Rock music originated in the rhythm and blues traditions of African Americans. Elvis Presley made rock music popular when he integrated African American gospel tunes into the music he played. Although some Americans complained about rock music, it nonetheless became a symbol of the emerging youth culture and of the growing power of youth on mass culture.

Hidden behind this prosperity were urban slums, desperate rural poverty, and discrimination. Michael Harrington's influential book *The Other America* (1962) opened Americans' eyes to the 50 million people, one fourth of the nation, living in poverty. Many of the "invisible" poor were inner-city African Americans, rural whites, and Latinos in migrant farm camps and urban barrios.

As the middle class moved from cities to the suburbs, cities lost revenue and political clout. Minorities moved in great numbers to cities in search of better economic opportunities. Strained city services, such as garbage removal, deteriorated. Crime increased in what was now called the inner city, further encouraging middle-class Americans to flee. Government-funded **urban renewal** projects tried to reverse this trend by creating developments that they hoped would revitalize downtowns. Many failed, pushing people from their homes into already overcrowded areas.

(Continues on the next page.)

Lesson Vocabulary

beatniks   small group of writers and artists, in the 1950s and early 1960s, who were critical of American society

rock-and-roll   popular music that grew out of the gospel and blues traditions of African Americans

urban renewal   government programs for redevelopment of urban areas

Lesson Summary
SOCIAL ISSUES OF THE 1950s (continued)

Many of the rural poor also relocated to cities. Small farmers slipped into poverty when they could not compete with corporations and large-farm owners dominating agricultural production.

Efforts to overcome housing and employment discrimination became central to the struggle for civil rights. Latinos and Native Americans struggled with many of the same problems. In 1953, the federal government enacted the **termination policy**, a law that sought to end tribal government and to relocate Native Americans to the nation's cities. Proponents of the policy argued that it would better enable American Indians to assimilate into American society.

Lesson Vocabulary

termination policy   a policy ending all programs monitored by the Bureau of Indian Affairs. It also ended federal responsibility for the health and welfare of Native Americans.

TOPIC 8 — Review Questions
POSTWAR AMERICA

Answer the questions below using the information in the Lesson Summaries on the previous pages.

Lesson 1: The Beginning of the Cold War

1. Which event proved that the policy of containment worked?

_____

_____

2. **Contrast** After World War II, what were the differences in goals between Stalin and the Soviets and Truman and the United States?

_____

_____

Lesson 2: The Korean War

3. **Categorize** What idea and event led directly to Truman's firing of MacArthur?

_____

_____

4. What is the significance of the 38th parallel?

_____

_____

Lesson 3: The Cold War Intensifies

5. **Identify Main Ideas** Describe the ways the United States and the Soviet Union competed with each other for supremacy.

_____

_____

6. How were brinksmanship and massive retaliation supposed to deter communist aggression?

_____

_____

Lesson 4: Cold War Fears at Home

7. How were the Smith Act and HUAC supposed to discourage communism in the United States?

_____

_____

8. **Identify Causes and Effects** Discuss the events that led to McCarthyism and the popularity of the senator from Wisconsin.

_____

_____

Lesson 5: Postwar Prosperity

9. What is the Taft-Hartley Act? Why was it passed?

_____

_____

10. Understand Effects How did the GI Bill benefit the American economy?

_____

_____

Lesson 6: Mass Culture in the 1950s

11. Discuss the factors that fostered suburban growth.

_____

_____

12. Identify Main Ideas Discuss changes in American education in the postwar period.

_____

_____

Lesson 7 Social Issues of the 1950s

13. Identify Main Ideas How did television and rock-and-roll impact postwar American society?

_____

_____

14. Discuss how cities changed during this period.

_____

_____

Name _____ Class _____ Date _____

Focus Question: In what ways did significant social change come to America in the 1960s?

As you read, note specific examples that support the idea that American society changed significantly during the 1960s.

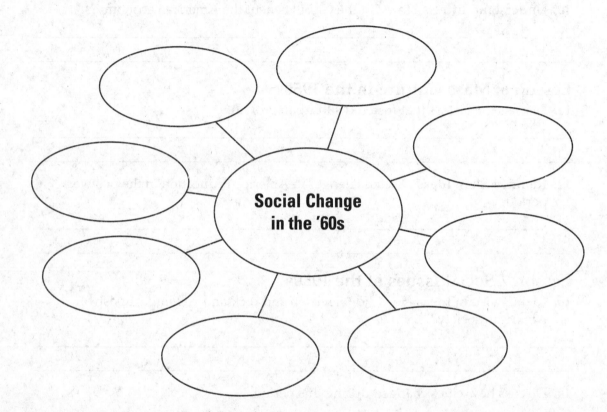

TOPIC 9 LESSON 1 — Lesson Summary
THE CIVIL RIGHTS MOVEMENT STRENGTHENS

After World War II, Jim Crow laws in the South continued to enforce strict separation of the races. Segregation that is imposed by law is known as **de jure segregation**. African Americans also faced segregation in the North, even where there were no explicit laws. **De facto segregation**, or segregation by unwritten custom, was a fact of life.

Thurgood Marshall, an African American lawyer, worked with civil rights organizations to challenge segregation in the courts. In 1954, *Brown* v. *Board of Education* challenged segregated public education at all grade levels. Chief Justice Earl Warren wrote the *Brown* decision in which the Supreme Court agreed that segregated public schools violated the United States Constitution. The *Brown* decision overturned the principle of "separate but equal." It also lent support to the view that all forms of segregation were wrong.

In Little Rock, Arkansas, the governor ordered the National Guard to block nine African American students from entering a high school. President Eisenhower sent federal troops to protect the students and to enforce the Court's decision. However, southern states continued to resist compliance with the law.

Congress passed the Civil Rights Act of 1957. This act established the U.S. Civil Rights Commission. The law's main significance was that it was the first civil rights bill passed by Congress since Reconstruction. It was a small, but important, victory.

In 1955, an African American woman named Rosa Parks refused to give up her bus seat to a white passenger in Montgomery, Alabama. She was arrested. A core of civil rights activists in Montgomery organized a one-day bus boycott to express opposition to Park's arrest and to segregation in general.

The next evening, Dr. Martin Luther King, Jr., a Baptist minister, gave an inspirational speech in which he called upon African Americans to protest segregation and oppression in a nonviolent manner. The Montgomery bus boycott continued for more than a year. In 1956, the Supreme Court ruled that the Montgomery city law that segregated buses was unconstitutional. The boycott revealed the power African Americans could have if they joined together. It also helped King and his philosophy of nonviolence to gain prominence within the civil rights movement.

Lesson Vocabulary

de jure segregation   segregation imposed by law

de facto segregation   segregation by unwritten custom or tradition

TOPIC 9 LESSON 2

Lesson Summary
THE MOVEMENT SURGES FORWARD

Despite some victories, activists continued to struggle for African Americans' civil rights. In North Carolina, four college students started a sit-in to protest discrimination. This **sit-in** sparked a wave of similar protests across the nation. Young African American activists established the Student Nonviolent Coordinating Committee (SNCC), to create a grass-roots movement to gain equality.

The next battleground was interstate transportation. The Supreme Court had ruled that segregation on interstate buses was illegal. In the spring of 1961, the Congress of Racial Equality (CORE) stage a **freedom ride** through the Deep South to test the federal government's willingness to enforce the law. After the freedom riders were met with violence, President John F. Kennedy intervened. Mississippi's leaders agreed to send police to protect the riders.

In September 1962, James Meredith won a federal court case that allowed him to enroll at the all-white University of Mississippi. Civil rights activist Medgar Evers was instrumental in this effort. Although full-scale riots erupted the night before his arrival, Meredith went on to graduate from the university in 1963.

In the spring of 1963, Martin Luther King, Jr., and the Southern Christian Leadership Conference (SCLC) targeted Birmingham, Alabama, for a major civil rights campaign. The campaign began nonviolently with protest marches and sit-ins. However, Birmingham's Public Safety Commissioner refused to tolerate the demonstrations. He used police dogs and fire hoses on the peaceful protesters. News coverage of the violence shocked many Americans.

To put pressure on Congress to pass a new civil rights bill, supporters organized a massive demonstration in Washington, D.C. More than 200,000 Americans gathered for the March on Washington on August 28, 1963. The highlight of the day came when King gave his "I Have a Dream" speech.

On November 22, 1963, President Kennedy was assassinated. Vice President Lyndon B. Johnson assumed the presidency. Johnson used his political skills to gain the passage of the Civil Rights Act of 1964, which banned segregation in public accommodations. The surge in support for the civil rights movement had produced a dramatic shift in race relations and set the stage for future reforms.

Lesson Vocabulary

sit-in   form of protest during which participants sit and refuse to move

freedom ride   1961 protest by activists who rode buses through southern states to test their compliance with laws banning segregation on interstate buses

TOPIC 9 LESSON 3

Lesson Summary
SUCCESSES AND SETBACKS

Although the civil rights movement had made progress, the southern political system still prevented African Americans from voting. In 1964, the SNCC mounted a major voter registration project, known as Freedom Summer. About 1,000 volunteers flooded Mississippi to register African Americans to vote.

In Selma, Alabama, Martin Luther King, Jr., and the SCLC organized a campaign to pressure the government to enact voting rights legislation. The protests climaxed in a series of confrontations, as heavily armed state troopers attacked the marchers. Spurred by the actions of the protesters, Congress passed the Voting Rights Act of 1965, which banned literacy tests. Another legal landmark was the Twenty-fourth Amendment, ratified in 1964. This amendment banned the poll tax, which had been used to prevent poor African Americans from voting.

Still, for some African Americans, things had not changed much. In many urban areas, anger over continuing discrimination and poverty erupted into violence and race riots. To determine the causes of the riots, President Johnson established the Kerner Commission. The commission concluded that long-term racial discrimination was the single most important cause of violence.

The riots coincided with the radicalization of many young urban African Americans. Malcolm X was the most well-known African American radical. Malcolm X became a prominent minister of the Nation of Islam, a religious sect that demanded separation of the races. However, he was assassinated in February 1965.

Many young African Americans considered themselves heirs of Malcolm X and moved away from the principle of nonviolence. SNCC leader Stokely Carmichael thought that African Americans should use their economic and political muscle, which he termed **"black power,"** to gain equality. Not long after, militants formed the Black Panther Party. Almost overnight, the Black Panthers became the symbol of young militant African Americans.

On April 4, 1968, Martin Luther King, Jr., was assassinated. In the wake of his murder, Congress passed the Fair Housing Act, which banned discrimination in housing. Although African Americans had made significant gains, the radicalism of the times left a bitter legacy.

Lesson Vocabulary

"black power"   economic and political muscle of African Americans

TOPIC
9
LESSON 4

Lesson Summary
KENNEDY'S REFORMS

MODIFIED CORNELL NOTES

The 1960 election featured Democrat John F. Kennedy and Republican Richard M. Nixon. Both were young, energetic, and intelligent. Kennedy won the election narrowly, in part due to an impressive performance in a televised debate.

President Kennedy promised Americans that his administration would blaze a "New Frontier." The term described Kennedy's proposals to improve the economy, education, healthcare, and civil rights. He used his charisma and a team of intelligent advisers to win support for his programs.

The high levels of poverty in America troubled Kennedy. Congress was hesitant to make reforms, but Kennedy did achieve an increase in the minimum wage and improvements in the welfare system. He also tried to make sure that women were paid equal wages for "equal work." The Equal Pay Act required this. Although it contained various loopholes, the law was an important step on the road to fair and equal employment practices.

The economy was weak when Kennedy took office, and he thought that improving the economy would reduce poverty. Kennedy accepted the "new economics" of John Maynard Keynes that advocated **deficit spending** to stimulate the economy. Deficit spending is the government practice of borrowing money in order to spend more than is received from taxes.

At first, Kennedy moved slowly on civil rights, worried that he would lose the support of the conservatives in his party. By 1963, however, Kennedy realized that African Americans needed the federal government to protect their rights. He introduced a bill that used federal money to aid school desegregation and demanded other reforms.

Perhaps the most visual component of the New Frontier was the active space program. Americans were afraid of falling behind the Soviets in the **"space race."** Kennedy called for a man to be landed on the moon in less than 10 years. That goal was met in 1969.

Kennedy's term as President was ended by his assassination. Lee Harvey Oswald shot Kennedy while he was riding in a car in Dallas, Texas. Although many people questioned whether Oswald acted alone, the Warren Commission, which conducted the official investigation of the shooting, declared that Oswald acted alone. The senseless murder deeply saddened Americans across the nation. It seemed as if part of America's innocence had died with Kennedy.

Lesson Vocabulary

deficit spending practice of a nation paying out more money than it is receiving in revenues

"space race" competition between the United States and the Soviet Union to successfully land on the moon

TOPIC 9 LESSON 5

Lesson Summary

REFORM UNDER JOHNSON

Lyndon B. Johnson, who became President after Kennedy's assassination, shared the same goals as his predecessor. Johnson's rise to the top was not easy. He was born in a small town in Texas. After attending a state college, he taught in a poor, segregated school for Mexican Americans. After teaching for several years, he was elected to Congress and began working his way up.

Johnson proved to be an excellent politician. One of his first successes after becoming President was ensuring that Congress passed the Civil Rights Act, an important bill introduced by President Kennedy. This bill was a major victory in the struggle to end discrimination in voting, education, and **public accommodations**.

The War on Poverty was a big part of Johnson's plans. He wanted to provide more training, education, and healthcare to those who needed it. The Economic Opportunity Act began this process by creating agencies such as Job Corps, VISTA, and Head Start.

After being elected President in 1964, Johnson called his vision for America the Great Society. He said the Great Society demanded "an end to poverty and racial injustice." In 1965, Congress began to pass Johnson's Great Society legislation.

One area of reform was in healthcare insurance. Johnson created Medicare, a program that provided basic hospital insurance for older Americans. He also created Medicaid, which provided basic medical services to poor and disabled Americans.

Education and immigration policy also saw reforms. The 1965 Elementary and Secondary Education Act aided schools in poorer communities. The Immigration and Nationality Act of 1965 relaxed the nation's immigration policies. Over the next two decades, millions of immigrants poured into the United States.

During the 1960s, the Supreme Court was also interested in reform. The court decided cases on controversial social, religious, and political issues. Led by Chief Justice Earl Warren—and often called the Warren Court—this liberal court supported civil rights, **civil liberties**, voting rights, and personal privacy.

Lesson Vocabulary

public accommodations   public or private establishments, such as schools, that are used by the public

civil liberties   freedom of the people from unwarranted government interference as guaranteed by the Bill of Rights

Name _____ Class _____ Date _____

Answer the questions below using the information in the Lesson Summaries on the previous pages.

Lesson 1: The Civil Rights Movement Strengthens

1. Explain the importance of *Brown* v. *Board of Education*.

_____

_____

2. **Summarize** List three key events of the 1950s that helped to end segregation.

_____

_____

Lesson 2: The Movement Surges Forward

3. What was the purpose of the March on Washington?

_____

_____

4. **Summarize** Summarize the significance of James Meredith's actions in 1962.

_____

_____

Lesson 3 Successes and Setbacks

5. Explain the significance of the march in Selma

_____

_____

6. **Summarize** Summarize the impact of Malcolm X on the civil rights movement.

_____

_____

Lesson 4: Kennedy's Reforms

7. What did Kennedy do to advance the space program?

_____

8. **Identify Main Ideas** What was deficit spending and why did Kennedy support it?

_____

_____

TOPIC 9 Review Questions
CIVIL RIGHTS AND REFORM IN THE 1960s (continued)

Lesson 5: Reform Under Johnson

9. **Identify Main Ideas** What did the Civil Rights Act accomplish?

_____

_____

10. What programs did Johnson create to fight poverty?

_____

_____

Name _____ Class _____ Date _____

Focus Question: Why were some people in favor of U.S. military involvement in Vietnam and other people against it?

As you read, take notes in the following chart to summarize the content of this topic. Note specific examples of reasons why people supported and opposed U.S. military involvement in Vietnam.

Supported	Opposed
•	•
•	•
	•

TOPIC 10 LESSON 1

Lesson Summary

THE COLD WAR AND VIETNAM

President Kennedy worked to build up the country's armed forces. He wanted a **flexible response** defense policy to prepare the United States to fight any size or any type of conflict. He also wanted to prevent the spread of communism in poor nations around the globe.

Kennedy's first major challenge came in Cuba. The revolutionary Fidel Castro took over Cuba in 1959 and aligned Cuba with the Soviet Union. Eisenhower had planned an invasion of Cuba to overthrow Castro, and Kennedy executed this plan in 1961. A CIA-led force of Cuban exiles attacked Cuba in the Bay of Pigs invasion. The invasion failed and probably ended up strengthening Castro's position in Cuba.

When the Soviets began building nuclear missile sites in Cuba in range of East Coast cities, Kennedy faced his third challenge. During the Cuban missile crisis, Kennedy demanded that the Soviets remove the missiles. Nuclear war seemed possible. After several tense days, Khrushchev agreed to remove the missiles. The leaders agreed to install a **hot line** telephone system between Moscow and Washington, D.C., to improve communication. A year later, in 1963, the United States, Great Britain, and the Soviet Union signed the first nuclear-weapons agreement.

Kennedy's next challenge involved the Soviet premier Nikita Khrushchev, who demanded that America remove its troops from West Berlin and recognize the divided city. Kennedy refused. Khrushchev then ordered the construction of a wall between East and West Berlin. The Berlin Wall became a symbol of the divide between communism and democracy.

France had controlled Vietnam as a colony since the 1800s. After World War II, however, a strong independence movement took hold. The movement was led by Ho Chi Minh, who had been fighting for Vietnamese independence for 30 years. Ho Chi Minh had fled Vietnam in 1912. During his travels around the world, he embraced communism and had formed ties with the Soviet Union.

(Continues on the next page.)

Lesson Vocabulary

flexible response   defense policy allowing for the appropriate action in any type of conflict

hot line   direct telephone line between the White House and the Kremlin set up after the Cuban Missile Crisis

Name _____ Class _____ Date _____

MODIFIED CORNELL NOTES

The United States became involved in Vietnam for several reasons. First, it wanted to keep France as an ally. To ensure French support in the Cold War, President Truman agreed to help France regain control over Vietnam. Second, both Truman and Eisenhower wanted to contain the spread of communism. They believed in the **domino theory**. This idea held that if Vietnam fell to communism, its closest neighbors would follow. Communism would then spread throughout the entire region.

The United States channeled aid to South Vietnam through the Southeast Asia Treaty Organization (SEATO).

In 1961, President Kennedy began sending U.S. troops to South Vietnam. President Johnson increased U.S. involvement after North Vietnam attacked a U.S. destroyer patrolling the Gulf of Tonkin. Congress passed the Gulf of Tonkin Resolution, which gave Johnson authority to use force to defend American troops. This resolution gave the President the power to commit U.S. troops to fight without asking Congress for a formal declaration of war.

Lesson Vocabulary

domino theory   idea that if a nation falls to communism, its closest neighbors will also fall under communist control

TOPIC 10
LESSON 2
Lesson Summary
AMERICA'S ROLE ESCALATES

In February 1965, President Johnson took the United States deeper into the Vietnam War by ordering a large bombing campaign called Operation Rolling Thunder. Despite massive and sustained airstrikes, communist forces continued to fight. Johnson then ordered more troops to fight them on the ground. This more active strategy came primarily from Secretary of Defense Robert McNamara and General William Westmoreland, the American commander in South Vietnam.

In addition to conventional bombs, American pilots dropped napalm and sprayed Agent Orange. **Napalm** is a jellied gasoline that covered large areas in flames. Agent Orange is an herbicide that destroys plant life. It was used to disrupt the enemy's food supply.

When the U.S. troops fought on the ground, it was rarely in large battles. The Vietcong and North Vietnamese Army fought with guerilla tactics in the jungle, trying to wear the United States down because they knew they could not win a traditional war. They followed Ho Chi Minh's doctrine, which stated that fighting should never be on the opponent's terms. Communist forces used hit-and-run attacks, nighttime ambushes, and booby traps. It was also difficult for the U.S. troops to know which Vietnamese person was a friend or an enemy.

By 1967, the war had become a stalemate. By 1968, more than 30,000 Americans had been killed in Vietnam. Despite the many times Johnson asserted that victory was near, each year yielded little progress. Troop morale began to fall.

The costs of the war had also grown each year, straining government finances. Government spending had lowered the unemployment rate at home, but it had also led to rising prices and inflation. President Johnson was forced to raise taxes, and social programs at home had to be cut.

The war was being questioned in Congress. In 1967, Congress was divided into two camps: hawks and doves. **Hawks** supported the war and believed they were fighting communism. **Doves** questioned the war on moral and strategic grounds. They were not convinced that Vietnam was a vital Cold War battleground.

Lesson Vocabulary

napalm   jellied gasoline dropped in canisters that explode on impact and cover large areas in flame; dropped by U.S. planes during the Vietnam War

hawk   person who supported U.S. involvement in the Vietnam War

dove   person who opposed U.S. involvement in the Vietnam War

Name _____ Class _____ Date _____

MODIFIED CORNELL NOTES

The war in Vietnam divided Americans and opened a deep emotional rift in American society. To provide enough soldiers for the war, the government drafted young men into service. Some of these **draftees**, however, thought that the selection method was unfair. Draft boards were allowed to grant deferments to college students and men who worked in certain occupations. The result was that most of the men who served in Vietnam came from working-class and poor backgrounds. The number of African Americans in Vietnam was also disproportionately high.

College campuses became centers of antiwar sentiment. The Students for a Democratic Society (SDS), formed in 1960 to fight racism and poverty, became a leading antiwar group. College students and police clashed during antiwar demonstrations. Nightly television coverage of the war fueled opposition to the conflict. The differences between war accounts given by journalists and the optimistic progress reported by the government created a **credibility gap**.

Because of the government's reports on the war, the public was greatly surprised by the Tet Offensive. This major offensive by the North Vietnamese Army showed that the enemy was still strong. The United States repelled the offensive, but after these attacks, American leaders seemed less confident of a quick end to the war.

Meanwhile, the 1968 election campaign began. Senator Eugene McCarthy, the antiwar Democratic presidential candidate, made a surprisingly strong showing in an early primary election. Democratic senator Robert Kennedy also announced his candidacy for President. Soon thereafter, Johnson announced that he would not run for another term as President.

The spring and summer of 1968 saw violence at home. First, civil rights leader Martin Luther King, Jr., was assassinated. Then, Robert Kennedy was assassinated after winning the California primary. In August, major protests erupted at the Democratic National Convention in Chicago. Police clashed with antiwar protesters in the streets outside the convention center. The chaos and civil disorder helped Republican Richard Nixon win the presidency in 1968. Nixon promised to achieve "peace with honor" in Vietnam.

Lesson Vocabulary

draftees   young American men drafted into military service

credibility gap   American public's growing distrust of statements made by the government during the Vietnam War

MODIFIED CORNELL NOTES

When Nixon became President, he believed that a peace deal could be negotiated with North Vietnam. However, when these negotiations stalled, Nixon gradually began to pull American troops out of Vietnam. He believed that the South Vietnamese army should fight on its own and called this approach **Vietnamization**. He hoped that sending American supplies to the South Vietnamese Army would be sufficient for the army to secure and hold South Vietnam.

In 1970, however, Nixon ordered a ground attack on communists in Cambodia, which angered antiwar activists at home. They claimed that Nixon was widening the war, not ending it. Protests erupted on many college campuses. At Kent State University, members of the National Guard fired into a crowd of protesters, killing four. This led to demonstrations on other campuses, including Jackson State in Mississippi, where two students were killed.

Other events also outraged the public. American troops killed more than 400 unarmed Vietnamese in the village of My Lai. The Pentagon Papers showed that the government had been dishonest with the public and with Congress about the Vietnam War.

American bombing finally induced the North Vietnamese to resume negotiations. In January 1973, the United States, South Vietnam, North Vietnam, and the Vietcong signed the Paris Peace Accords. American troops would withdraw from South Vietnam, and North Vietnamese troops would remain in South Vietnam. The war was over for the United States, but the fighting continued in Vietnam. The Soviet-supplied North Vietnamese Army defeated the South Vietnamese Army, and Vietnam was united under a communist regime.

More than 58,000 American troops and over 2 million Vietnamese had been killed in the Vietnam War. Turmoil troubled Southeast Asia for many years afterward. After the difficult experience in Vietnam, Americans were less willing to intervene in the affairs of other countries. Americans also had less trust in their leaders. In 1973, Congress passed the War Powers Act, which restricted the President's authority to commit American troops to foreign conflicts. The fear of "another Vietnam" would affect American foreign policy for decades to come.

Lesson Vocabulary

Vietnamization   President Nixon's plan for gradual withdrawal of U.S. forces as South Vietnamese troops assumed more combat duties

Name _____ Class _____ Date _____

Answer the questions below using the information in the Lesson Summaries on the previous pages.

Lesson 1: The Cold War and Vietnam

1. **Summarize** Why did the United States help France in Vietnam?

_____

_____

2. What was the domino theory?

_____

_____

Lesson 2: America's Role Escalates

3. Which group in Congress opposed the war in Vietnam?

_____

_____

4. **Identify Supporting Details** Why did President Johnson raise taxes?

_____

_____

Lesson 3: The Antiwar Movement

5. Why did some people think that the draft system was unfair?

_____

_____

6. **Recognize Sequence** How did the protests at the Democratic National Convention in 1968 help Richard Nixon?

_____

_____

Lesson 4: The War's End and Effects

7. Why did the Pentagon Papers outrage Americans?

_____

_____

8. **Recognize Effects** What was one effect of the Vietnam War on American foreign policy?

_____

_____

Name _____ Class _____ Date _____

Note Taking Study Guide

AN ERA OF CHANGE

Focus Question: How did the activist movements of the 1960s and 1970s shape America?

As you read, take notes in the chart below. Note one specific example of what each of the activist movements described in this Topic achieved in the 1960s and 1970s.

Activist Movements and Achievements			
Movement:	Movement:	Movement:	Movement:
Achievements:	Achievements:	Achievements:	Achievements:

TOPIC 11 LESSON 1

Lesson Summary
THE COUNTERCULTURE OF THE 1960s

The **counterculture** grew out of the Beat movement's emphasis on freedom from materialism and the civil rights movement's questioning of traditional boundaries. The antiwar movement's distrust of authority, sparked by the Vietnam War, fostered a spirit of rebellion. Members of the counterculture, known as hippies, valued youth, spontaneity, and individuality, and promoted peace, love, and freedom. Their experimentation with drugs, new styles of dress and music, and freer attitudes toward sexual relationships contradicted traditional values and boundaries. This rebellion led to a misunderstanding between the older and younger generation, a situation that was called a **generation gap**.

Born after World War II, the younger generation had an enormous influence on American society, driving changes in attitudes and styles in everything from clothes to music and art. Rock-and-roll music by bands such as the Beatles came to define the decade. Hippies rejected many traditional restrictions on sexual behavior in what became known as the "sexual revolution." Many also often adopted new living patterns, residing in **communes**, small communities where people shared interests and resources.

The center of the counterculture was the Haight-Ashbury district of San Francisco. There, hippies experimented with drugs and listened to rock music and speeches by political radicals such as Timothy Leary, who encouraged youths to "tune in," "turn on" to drugs, and "drop out" of mainstream society.

Some hippies sought spirituality outside of the Judeo-Christian tradition, exploring Eastern religions and practices of Native Americans. Some sought to live off the land in harmony with nature. These beliefs impacted the growing environmental movement.

By the late 1960s, several key figures of the counterculture died from drug overdoses, and many people had become disillusioned with the movement's excesses. Most hippies eventually rejoined the mainstream, but the seeds of protest sown during the 1960s would influence the growing "rights revolution."

Lesson Vocabulary

counterculture movement that upheld values different from those of mainstream culture

generation gap lack of understanding and communication between older and younger members of society

communes small communities where people with common interests live and share resources

TOPIC
11
LESSON 2

Lesson Summary
THE WOMEN'S RIGHTS MOVEMENT

The first wave of feminism began in the 1840s and culminated in 1920 with women winning the right to vote. **Feminism** is the theory of political, social, and economic equality for men and women. The second wave of feminism was born in the 1960s. Inspired by successes of the civil rights movement, women wanted to change how they were treated as a group and to redefine how they were viewed as individuals.

The role of housewife was seen as the proper one for women, but many women found it deeply unsatisfying. Those women who did work experienced open and routine discrimination, including being paid less than men. Betty Friedan described women's dissatisfaction in her 1963 book *The Feminine Mystique*. Friedan later helped establish the National Organization for Women (NOW), which sought to win equality for women. The group campaigned for passage of the Equal Rights Amendment (ERA), an amendment to the Constitution that would guarantee gender equality under the law. NOW also worked to protect women's right to abortions. Radical feminists went further, conducting protests to expose discrimination against women. One radical feminist was Gloria Steinem, who sought to raise consciousness through the media and helped co-found *Ms.* magazine in 1972.

Not all women supported these efforts. Phyllis Schlafly, a conservative political activist, denounced women's liberation as "a total assault on the family, on marriage, and on children." The ERA failed to pass partly due to her efforts.

Women did, however, gain new legal rights. Title IX of the Higher Education Act of 1972 banned discrimination in education and the Equal Credit Opportunity Act made it illegal to deny credit to a woman on the basis of gender. The 1973 Supreme Court decision in *Roe* v. *Wade* gave women the right to legal abortions.

Changes in the workplace came slowly. Today, more women work, and more work in fields such as medicine and law that were once restricted to them. Despite these gains, the average woman still earns less than the average man, partly because women continue to work in fields that pay less.

Lesson Vocabulary

feminism   theory that women and men should have political, social, and economic equality

Lesson Summary
EXPANDING THE PUSH FOR EQUALITY

MODIFIED CORNELL NOTES

Mexican and other Latin American immigrants came to the United States during and after World War II, filling the need for cheap labor. Mexican immigrants came as temporary farmworkers. Other immigrants came from Puerto Rico, Cuba, and the Dominican Republic. The bracero program allowed Mexicans to work on American farms. After passage of the Immigration and Nationality Act Amendments in 1965, immigration from Latin America surged.

Following the lead of the civil rights movement, Latinos began fighting for their rights. The most influential Latino activist was Cesar Chavez, who formed the United Farm Workers (UFW). This union implemented a strike and boycott of grapes that secured safer working conditions for **migrant farmworkers**. These workers were often exploited as they moved from farm to farm to pick fruits and vegetables. A broader movement known as the **Chicano movement** worked to raise consciousness, reduce poverty and discrimination, and attain political power for Latinos.

Native Americans formed their own protest groups. One group took over the island of Alcatraz and claimed it for the Sioux. Another group, the American Indian Movement (AIM), was founded in 1968 to ease poverty and help secure legal rights and self-government for Native Americans. In February 1973, AIM took over Wounded Knee, South Dakota, to protest living conditions on reservations. That protest led to the deaths of two AIM members. Laws helping Native Americans were passed in the 1970s, including the Indian Self-Determination Act of 1975, which granted tribes greater control over resources on reservations.

The consumer rights movement started after Ralph Nader published *Unsafe at Any Speed*, a book that investigated the link between flawed car design and deaths in automobile accidents. The book prompted Congress to pass laws to improve automobile safety. Americans with disabilities, due in part to activism by Korean and Vietnam War veterans, also secured additional rights. Several laws were passed in the 1970s guaranteeing equal access to education for those with disabilities.

Lesson Vocabulary

migrant farmworkers   people who travel from farm to farm to pick fruits and vegetables

Chicano movement   movement to promote Mexican American social and political issues and culture

TOPIC 11 LESSON 4 — Lesson Summary
THE ENVIRONMENTAL MOVEMENT

Published in 1962, Rachel Carson's *Silent Spring* inspired much environmental activism. The book describes the deadly impact that pesticides were having on birds and other animals. Carson argued that humans were drastically altering the environment and had a responsibility to protect it. Protests sparked by the book eventually compelled Congress to restrict use of the pesticide DDT.

Other environmental concerns included toxic waste such as coal smog—poisonous **byproducts** of human activity. One response to environmental concerns was Earth Day. Close to 20 million Americans took part in the first Earth Day, held on April 22, 1970, and it has since become an annual event.

Public outcry over environmental issues convinced President Nixon to support environmental reforms. Under his leadership, Congress created the Environmental Protection Agency (EPA) in 1970 to protect "the entire ecological chain." The EPA worked to clean up and protect the environment and sought to limit or eliminate pollutants that posed a risk to the public's health. Nixon also signed a number of environmental laws. The Clean Air Act (1970) combated air pollution by limiting the **emissions** from factories and automobiles. The Clean Water Act (1973) reduced water pollution by industry and agriculture. The Endangered Species Act (1973) helped to protect endangered plants and animals.

In the late 1970s, several crises reinforced the public's environmental concern. Toxic waste in the ground was blamed for high rates of birth defects and cancer in Love Canal, New York. Later, a nuclear reactor at Three Mile Island in Pennsylvania malfunctioned and the core began to melt.

While these events solidified some people's support for environmental regulation, other people questioned and opposed the government's actions. Conservatives complained that regulation took away individuals' property rights. Others argued that private property owners, rather than the government, should protect the environment. Industry leaders worried that too much environmental regulation would harm business.

Lesson Vocabulary

byproduct   additional material created during manufacturing or industrial production of a primary product

emission   the act or instance of discharging a substance

TOPIC
11
LESSON 5

Lesson Summary

THE TWO SIDES OF THE NIXON PRESIDENCY

MODIFIED CORNELL NOTES

During his years as President, Richard Nixon fundamentally reshaped the way the United States approached the world. His leading adviser on national security and international affairs, Henry Kissinger, helped him.

In foreign affairs, Nixon and Kissinger shared the idea of **realpolitik**, a German word meaning "real politics." According to this idea, a nation's political goals around the world should be defined by what is good for the nation instead of by abstract ideologies.

In 1972, Nixon traveled to China and met with Premier Zhou Enlai and Chairman Mao Zedong. The visit was a historic first step toward normalizing relations between the two countries.

Nixon's trip to China was met by an immediate reaction from the Soviet Union. Soviet leader Leonid Brezhnev invited the President to visit Moscow, where they signed the first Strategic Arms Limitation Treaty. This agreement froze the deployment of intercontinental ballistic missiles and placed limits on antiballistic missiles. The treaty was a first step toward limiting the arms race.

The United States and Soviet Union now implemented a new policy called **détente** to replace the prior foreign policy, which was based on suspicion and distrust. Détente eased tensions between the two nations.

In 1968, Richard Nixon narrowly defeated Democrat Hubert Humphrey to win the presidency. During the campaign, Nixon claimed to represent the **silent majority**, the working men and women who made up middle America. He believed that they were tired of "big" government.

(Continues on the next page.)

Lesson Vocabulary

realpolitik   a foreign policy based on concrete national interests instead of abstract ideologies; promoted by Henry Kissinger during the Nixon administration

détente   flexible diplomacy adopted by President Richard Nixon to ease tensions between the United States, the Soviet Union, and the People's Republic of China

silent majority   phrase introduced by President Richard Nixon to refer to a significant number of Americans who supported his policies but chose to not express their views

TOPIC 11 · LESSON 5

Lesson Summary

THE TWO SIDES OF THE NIXON PRESIDENCY (continued)

Nixon's presidency was plagued by a combination of recession and inflation that came to be known as **stagflation**. When the Organization of Petroleum Exporting Countries (OPEC) placed an oil embargo on Israel's allies, oil prices skyrocketed.

Nixon set out to expand his base of support. His **southern strategy** targeted southern whites, who had traditionally voted for Democrats.

In June 1972, burglars broke into the Democratic Party headquarters at the Watergate complex in Washington. After their conviction, one of them charged that administration officials had been involved. Nixon denied any wrongdoing in what came to be known as the Watergate scandal.

He claimed **executive privilege**, which is the principle that the President has the right to keep certain information confidential. However, the Supreme Court ordered Nixon to turn over the tapes. These tapes provided evidence of Nixon's involvement in the coverup. In order to avoid impeachment and conviction, Nixon resigned in August 1974.

Lesson Vocabulary

stagflation   term for the economic condition created in the late 1960s and 1970s by high inflation combined with stagnant economic growth and high unemployment

southern strategy   tactic of the Republican Party to win presidential elections by securing the electoral votes of southern states

executive privilege   principle that the President has the right to keep private certain communications between himself and other members of the executive branch

MODIFIED CORNELL NOTES

Lesson Summary

FORD AND CARTER STRUGGLE

Gerald Ford had a long record of public service. When he became President after Nixon's resignation, he had the support of Democrats as well as Republicans. However, he lost support when he announced that he had **pardoned**, or officially forgiven, Nixon for any crimes he might have committed as President.

Relations with the Soviet Union were central to U.S. foreign policy during the Ford and Carter administrations. President Gerald Ford and Soviet leader Leonid Brezhnev met twice and endorsed the Helsinki Accords. In this document, the nations of Europe expressed their support of **human rights**. However, Ford chose to put arms control ahead of human rights. The United States continued disarmament talks with the Soviets.

Former Georgia governor Jimmy Carter won the presidency in the 1976 election. A day after his inauguration, he granted **amnesty** to Americans who had evaded the draft, in the hope of moving the nation beyond the Vietnam War. Severe inflation continued, fueled by the ongoing energy crisis.

Early in his presidency, Jimmy Carter announced that his foreign policy would be guided by a concern for human rights. He tried to use his foreign policy to end acts of political repression, such as torture. Carter also worked to achieve détente, and in 1979, he signed the SALT II treaty to limit nuclear arms production. However, relations between the two superpowers took a frosty turn after the Soviet Union invaded Afghanistan in December 1979. Carter responded by imposing **sanctions** on the Soviets, including a boycott of the 1980 Summer Olympic Games in Moscow. Carter also hoped to change the way the United States dealt with the **developing world**. His emphasis on human rights led him to alter the U.S. relationship with a number of dictators.

(Continues on the next page.)

Lesson Vocabulary

pardoned   official forgiveness of a crime and its punishment

human rights   basic rights held by every human being, including religious freedom, education, and equality

amnesty   general pardon for certain crimes

sanctions   penalties intended to make people obey laws and rules, especially measures taken to force a country to obey international law

developing world   countries that are less economically advanced than developed countries such as the United States and those of Western Europe

TOPIC 11
LESSON 6

Lesson Summary
FORD AND CARTER STRUGGLE (continued)

Carter's greatest foreign policy success and setback were both in the Middle East. Egypt and Israel had been enemies since Israel's founding in 1948. In 1977, Carter invited the leaders of the two nations to the presidential retreat. The result was the Camp David Accords, which led to a peace treaty in which Egypt recognized Israel.

The 1970s also witnessed a resurgence of fundamental Christianity. **Televangelists** such as Jerry Falwell preached to millions on television. Religious conservatives opposed many of the social changes that begun in the 1960s and had gone mainstream in the 1970s. They began to form alliances with other conservatives to forge a new political majority.

Lesson Vocabulary

televangelists   ministers who use the television to preach

TOPIC 11 Review Questions
AN ERA OF CHANGE

Answer the questions below using the information in the Lesson Summaries on the previous pages.

Lesson 1: The Counterculture of the 1960s

1. **Identify Main Ideas** How did social and political events help shape the counterculture?

_____

_____

2. What district in San Francisco was at the center of the counterculture?

_____

_____

Lesson 2: The Women's Rights Movement

3. **Cause and Effect** What inspired the second wave of feminism?

_____

_____

4. **Cause and Effect** What causes did the National Organization for Women work toward? Did its efforts succeed or fail?

_____

_____

Lesson 3: Expanding the Push for Equality

5. What organization did Cesar Chavez help organize?

_____

_____

6. **Compare and Contrast** Compare and contrast the goals of the United Farm Workers and the Chicano Movement.

_____

_____

Lesson 4: The Environmental Movement

7. What agency works to limit or eliminate pollution?

_____

_____

8. **Recognize Sequence** Which two events preceded President Nixon's environmental reforms?

_____

_____

TOPIC 11 Review Questions
AN ERA OF CHANGE (continued)

Lesson 5: The Two Sides of the Nixon Presidency

9. Identify Main Ideas How did Nixon improve relations between the United States and China, as well as the United States and the Soviet Union?

_____

_____

10. Why did President Nixon resign as president in 1974?

_____

_____

Lesson 6: Ford and Carter Struggle

11. What did President Ford prioritize over human rights?

_____

_____

12. What was President Carter's guiding principle for his foreign policy?

_____

_____

TOPIC 12 Note Taking Study Guide

AMERICA IN THE 1980s AND 1990s

Focus Question: What were the major domestic and foreign policy issues during the 1980s and 1990s?

As you read, note specific examples of domestic and foreign policies implemented by Presidents Reagan, Bush, and Clinton.

I. Ronald Reagan

    A. Domestic _____

        1. _____

        2. _____

    B. Foreign Policy _____

        1. _____

        2. _____

II. _____

    A. Domestic _____

    B. Foreign Policy _____

        1. _____

        2. _____

III. _____

    A. Domestic _____

        1. _____

        2. _____

    B. Foreign Policy _____

        1. _____

        2. _____

TOPIC 12 LESSON 1 — Lesson Summary
THE CONSERVATIVE MOVEMENT SURGES

The two major political parties in the late twentieth century were the Democrats, many of whom were "liberals," and the Republicans, often labeled "conservatives." **Liberals** believed that the federal government should play an active role in improving the lives of all Americans. They supported social programs and government regulation of industry, and favored cooperation with international organizations such as the United Nations.

Conservatives believed that the free market, private organizations, and individuals, instead of the government, should care for the needy. They opposed big government, favored tax cuts, and supported a strong military.

Many things contributed to the conservative movement known as the New Right, which grew rapidly during the 1960s and 1970s. The Vietnam War and urban riots of the 1960s divided the country. The counterculture had alienated many Americans. Watergate, the oil crises of the 1970s, and the Iran hostage crisis further weakened the public's faith in the federal government. When the economy stagnated, conservative beliefs became more attractive.

Conservatives blamed liberal policies for the economic problems of the late 1970s. They believed that the government taxed too heavily and spent too much money on the wrong programs. They complained about **unfunded mandates**, programs required but not paid for by the federal government.

In 1979, Reverend Jerry Falwell founded the Moral Majority, a political organization based on religious beliefs. Its supporters worried about the decline of the traditional family. They were also concerned that the new freedoms brought by the counterculture would lead to the degeneration of modern youth.

The conservative movement swept the Republican presidential candidate, former actor and two-term California governor Ronald Reagan, to victory over Democratic incumbent Jimmy Carter in the 1980 election. Reagan's conservative beliefs, charm, and optimism convinced Americans that he would usher in a new era of prosperity and patriotism.

Lesson Vocabulary

liberals people who tend to support government intervention to help the needy and favors laws protecting the rights of women and minorities

conservatives people who tend to support limited government involvement in the economy, community help for the needy, and traditional values

unfunded mandates program or action required but not paid for by the federal government

Name _____ Class _____ Date _____

MODIFIED CORNELL NOTES

President Reagan's economic policies, or "Reaganomics," were based on the theory of **supply-side economics**, which assumes that reducing taxes gives more people more incentive to work and more money to spend, causing the economy to grow. The government would then collect more tax dollars without raising taxes. Congress passed the Economic Recovery Act of 1981, which reduced taxes by 25 percent over three years.

Reagan called for **deregulation**, or the removal of government control over industries, including airline and telecommunications industries. He also appointed conservative judges to federal courts.

The economy experienced a severe recession from 1980 through 1982 but rebounded in 1983. Inflation fell and the Gross National Product increased. Still, the number of poor increased and the richest grew even richer. Reagan increased defense spending but failed to win cuts in other areas of the budget, leading to a **budget deficit**, a shortfall between money spent and money collected by the government. The **national debt**, the amount of money the government owes to owners of government bonds, also rose. Deficit problems worsened when the government had to bail out depositors of the nearly one thousand Savings and Loan banks that failed in the Savings and Loan (S&L) crisis of 1989.

Reagan faced other problems. American students were scoring lower on standardized tests, prompting conservatives to further lobby for **vouchers**, or government checks that could be used by parents to pay tuition at private schools. The nation also faced a new disease—Acquired Immunodeficiency Syndrome (AIDS). By the end of the 1980s, AIDS was the biggest killer of men between the ages of 20 and 40.

Despite these problems, Reagan remained popular and was overwhelmingly reelected in 1984. However, his momentum did not lead to a triumph for conservatives in Congress. Democrats retained control of the House of Representatives.

Lesson Vocabulary

supply-side economics   economic theory which says that reducing tax rates stimulates economic growth

deregulation   reduction or removal of government controls over an industry, based on the belief that more freedom leads to greater success and profitability

budget deficit   shortfall between the amount of money spent and the amount of money taken in by the federal government

national debt   total amount of money that the federal government owes to the holders of government bonds

voucher   certificate or other document that can be used in place of money

TOPIC 12 LESSON 3 — Lesson Summary
THE COLD WAR ENDS

Under President Reagan, the United States worked to weaken communism and the Soviet Union by committing to the largest peacetime military buildup in its history. Reagan believed that the Soviet Union would be unable to match U.S. defense spending. Reagan also proposed the Strategic Defense Initiative (SDI), which would use lasers to destroy missiles aimed at the United States. Furthermore, Reagan supported anticommunist rebellions world-wide, including the Contras, anticommunist counterrevolutionaries in Nicaragua.

Mikhail Gorbachev, who became the leader of the Soviet Union in 1985, initiated reforms to move the country away from a state-controlled economy. He pursued the policies of *glasnost*, meaning a new openness, and *perestroika*, reforming the Soviet system. As Reagan predicted, Gorbachev realized that the Soviet Union could not match the U.S. military buildup. Relations between the two nations improved. Both eventually signed a nuclear arms pact and began negotiating for a reduction of nuclear weapons.

The Cold War came to an end. The Berlin Wall tumbled in November 1989. From 1989 through 1991, communists lost power in Poland, Hungary, Czechoslovakia, Bulgaria, Romania, Albania, and Yugoslavia. And the Soviet Union split into 15 independent republics when it collapsed in 1991.

In the Middle East, 241 United States Marines stationed in Lebanon were killed by a truck bomb. The United States repeatedly clashed with Libya, whose leader, Muammar al-Qaddafi, supported terrorist groups. One breakthrough in Middle East affairs, minutes into Reagan's presidency, was the release of all 52 American hostages held by Iran. However, Reagan's second term was tarnished by the Iran-Contra affair. In 1985, the United States sold weapons to Iran in exchange for Iran's promise to pressure Lebanese terrorists to release American hostages, contradicting the administration's policy of refusing to negotiate with terrorists. Money from this sale was then used to fund Contras in Nicaragua, despite a congressional ban on such funding. Ultimately, several top officials were convicted of charges stemming from the scandal.

Lesson Vocabulary

glasnost   Russian term for "new openness," a policy in the Soviet Union in the 1980s calling for open discussion of national problems

perestroika   policy in the Soviet Union in the late 1980s calling for restructuring of the stagnant Soviet economy

TOPIC 12 LESSON 4

Lesson Summary
A NEW ERA IN FOREIGN POLICY

Under President George H.W. Bush, the United States took a leading role in world affairs. Bush continued the war on drugs, and in December 1989, U.S. troops invaded Panama and arrested its dictator, Manuel Noriega. Noriega was convicted of drug trafficking and sentenced to 40 years in an American prison.

Iraq's invasion of Kuwait in August 1990 was one of Bush's greatest foreign policy challenges. Saddam Hussein, Iraq's dictator, sought to control Kuwait's rich oil deposits and increase his power in the region.

President Bush made it clear that he would not tolerate Iraq's aggression against its neighbor. He worked to build an international coalition and backed a United Nations resolution demanding that Iraqi troops withdraw. Hussein did not comply. Under the name Operation Desert Storm, American, British, French, Egyptian, and Saudi coalition forces attacked Iraqi troops on January 16, 1991.

Twelve years after the Reagan Revolution, Americans were ready for a change in the White House. The Democrats nominated William Jefferson Clinton, governor of Arkansas, to run against President Bush in the 1992 election. Texas billionaire H. Ross Perot ran as an independent. Clinton carried the election, and Democrats retained control of both houses of Congress.

On the political scene, many Americans opposed military involvement in foreign affairs, but Clinton found it necessary to intervene in conflicts in Somalia and Haiti. When civil war broke out in the former Yugoslav republic of Bosnia, Bosnian Serbs attacked and murdered Muslims and Croats. This state-sanctioned mass murder became known as **ethnic cleansing**. In 1995, Clinton asked NATO to bomb Serbian strongholds. This intervention brought about a cease-fire, but violence flared in another former Yugoslavian republic. NATO troops, including U.S. troops, responded again.

The ongoing conflict between Israelis and Palestinians escalated in the 1990s. Clinton led negotiations that produced a short-lived agreement between Israeli and Palestinian leaders. That involvement in the Middle East made the United States a target of a terrorist group called al Qaeda. The group launched several attacks on U.S. targets at home and abroad.

Lesson Vocabulary

ethnic cleansing   systematic effort to purge a society of an ethnic group through murder or deportation

TOPIC 12 LESSON 5 — Lesson Summary
CLINTON AND THE 1990S

Early in his presidency, Clinton focused on domestic issues. He signed the Family Medical Leave Act, which guaranteed most full-time employees unpaid leave each year for personal or family medical reasons. Clinton also oversaw passage of the Brady Bill, which placed a five-day waiting period on sales of handguns. Another important issue for Clinton was healthcare reform. Clinton's wife, Hillary, led a task force to investigate ways to guarantee healthcare for all Americans. The committee's proposal never won congressional support and was ultimately dropped.

In the 1994 midterm election, Georgia congressman Newt Gingrich led the opposition to Clinton. He galvanized Republicans around his Contract With America, a plan that attacked big government and emphasized patriotism and traditional values. Winning the votes of Americans who felt the federal government was too big, too wasteful, and too liberal, Republicans captured the House, the Senate, and most state governorships.

President Clinton had dodged scandals from his first day in office. One concerned investments the Clintons had made. Special prosecutor Kenneth Starr investigated the case for seven years but failed to uncover evidence of the Clintons' guilt. In the process, however, Starr investigated the President's relationship with a White House intern. When Clinton admitted he had lied about his affair with the intern under oath, Starr recommended **impeachment** proceedings. The House of Representatives impeached Clinton on the charges of perjury and obstruction of justice. Clinton was tried and acquitted by the Senate in February 1999.

The rapid pace of technological change in the twentieth century touched every aspect of modern life. One of the most important innovations was the computer. The first modern computer was developed in 1946 and filled an entire basement. As technology improved, small computers called personal computers were introduced. By the 1980s, **personal computers** were transforming American business and industry. They also changed medical science and helped create a new field called **biotechnology**, in which technology is used to solve problems affecting living organisms.

(Continues on the next page.)

Lesson Vocabulary

impeachment   accusation against a public official of wrongdoing in office

personal computer   small computer intended for individual use

biotechnology   application of technology to solve problems affecting living organisms

Lesson Summary

CLINTON AND THE 1990S (continued)

MODIFIED CORNELL NOTES

The late twentieth century ushered in the "information age." **Satellites** orbiting Earth increased the speed of global communications. Cellular telephones using satellite technology enabled people to communicate away from their homes. By the 1990s, the Internet made communication and access to information almost instantaneous, which in turn profoundly altered commerce, education, research, and entertainment.

Lesson Vocabulary

satellite   mechanical device that orbits Earth, receiving and sending communication signals or transmitting scientific data

TOPIC 12 **Review Questions**

AMERICA IN THE 1980s AND 1990s

Answer the questions below using the information in the Lesson Summaries on the previous pages.

Lesson 1: The Conservative Movement Surges

1. Summarize Describe the differences between the liberal and conservative viewpoints of government.

_____

_____

2. What events contributed to the rise of conservatism?

_____

_____

Lesson 2: The Reagan Era

3. Identify Main Ideas Describe the central idea of Reagan's economic policies.

_____

_____

4. What occurred in the economy during the early 1980s?

_____

_____

Lesson 3: The Cold War Ends

5. Sequence Describe Mikhail Gorbachev's policies that brought reform to the Soviet Union prior to the collapse of communism.

_____

_____

6. Why did the Iran-Contra affair tarnish President Reagan's presidency?

_____

_____

Lesson 4: A New Era in Foreign Policy

7. Summarize Summarize President Bush's approach to Iraq's aggression toward Kuwait?

_____

_____

8. Why did President Clinton ask NATO to bomb Serbian strongholds?

_____

_____

TOPIC 12

Review Questions

AMERICA IN THE 1980s AND 1990s (continued)

Lesson 5: Clinton and the 1990s

9. **Summarize** Summarize the difficulties President Clinton faced during his two terms in office.

_____

_____

10. What transformed American business and industry in the 1980s?

_____

_____

TOPIC 13

Note Taking Study Guide

AMERICA IN THE TWENTY-FIRST CENTURY

Focus Question: How have modern-day U.S presidents handled domestic and foreign issues?

As you read, take notes about the domestic and foreign policy issues faced by modern-day U.S. presidents in the chart below. Note the main challenge, or problem, each U.S. president faced and how he attempted to solve the problem.

Problems	Solutions
•	•
•	•
•	•

TOPIC 13 LESSON 1

Lesson Summary

AMERICA AND THE WORLD ECONOMY

In the 1990s, the United States was the world's sole superpower, wielding influence over economic and political events worldwide. Among the issues influenced by the United States was free trade. The European Union (EU), which coordinates monetary and economic policies among European nations, is an example of a free trade bloc. When the EU threatened U.S. economic leadership, the United States joined with Canada and Mexico to pass the North American Free Trade Agreement (NAFTA). NAFTA created a free trade zone in North America.

Clinton supported NAFTA and other free trade agreements, although many Democrats didn't. In 1994, he signed the revision to the General Agreement on Tariffs and Trade (GATT) aimed at reducing tariffs worldwide. In 1995, he signed the accords of the World Trade Organization (WTO), which replaced GATT and had greater authority to negotiate agreements and settle disputes.

Technological changes influenced how and where people worked. Fewer Americans worked in factories or on farms. Instead, they provided services. Satellites and computers increased **globalization**, the process by which national economies, politics, cultures, and societies become integrated with those of other nations around the world. A **multinational corporation** might have its financial headquarters in one country and manufacturing plants in several other countries. It might get raw materials from many different places and sell its products to a worldwide market.

Some economists say that the United States now has a **service economy**. Jobs in the service sector vary widely, from some of the highest paying, such as lawyers, to some of the lowest paying, such as fast-food workers. With the rise of the service economy and the decline of industries such as mining and manufacturing, the political power of labor unions has decreased and the average wages of workers have fallen.

Lesson Vocabulary

globalization   process by which national economies, politics, cultures, and societies mix with those of other nations around the world

multinational corporation   company that produces and sells their goods and services all over the world

service economy   economic system focused on the buying and selling of services

TOPIC 13 LESSON 2 — Lesson Summary
THE GEORGE W. BUSH PRESIDENCY

In the 2000 presidential election, Democrat Al Gore, Jr., ran against Republican George W. Bush. The results of the election were disputed. Democrats demanded a recount in Florida, where the vote was very close. Republicans sued to prevent the recount. The Supreme Court ended the recount and Bush won.

President Bush's domestic agenda focused on the economy and education. In 2002, Congress passed the No Child Left Behind Act. This penalized schools that did not reach federal performance standards and also called for improving teacher quality. He also promised to reform Social Security and Medicare. Although some progress was made with the Medicare Act of 2003, Democrats opposed Bush's reforms to Social Security.

On September 11, 2001, terrorists from the group al Qaeda launched a deadly attack against the United States. President Bush declared a war on terrorism. The Islamic fundamentalist Taliban government of Afghanistan refused to turn over al Qaeda leader Osama bin Laden. Bush then sent forces into Afghanistan. The Taliban was overthrown, but bin Laden escaped.

At home, improving national security became a priority. The Patriot Act gave law enforcement broader powers to monitor suspected terrorists. A new Cabinet-level Department of Homeland Security coordinated domestic security matters.

Bush turned his attention to Iraq. He asserted that Iraqi dictator Saddam Hussein had **weapons of mass destruction** and was a threat to U.S. security. In March 2003, American and British military forces invaded Iraq and soon toppled Saddam. However, violence erupted between ethnic groups and against American troops. In his second term, Bush's approval rating fell, and Democrats gained control of Congress. Voters became even more dissatisfied after a major financial crisis began in 2008.

Lesson Vocabulary

weapons of mass destruction   nuclear, biological, and chemical weapons intended to kill or harm on a large scale

TOPIC 13 — LESSON 3

Lesson Summary
THE BARACK OBAMA PRESIDENCY

MODIFIED CORNELL NOTES

In 2008, Democrat Barack Obama was elected as the first African American President. He ran against Republican nominee John McCain, a senator from Arizona. The two candidates had come from very different backgrounds. McCain was a former pilot and prisoner of war during the Vietnam War. He had served in Congress since 1982. Obama had served in the Illinois state legislature before being elected to the United States Senate. He had also been a community organizer in Chicago. The election drew a large voter turnout, with the majority of people citing the economy as their main concern.

Obama launched a stimulus package that pumped billions of dollars into the economy. Obama also ended the U.S. military mission in Iraq, focusing instead on the war in Afghanistan.

Obama also pursued healthcare reform. During his campaign, he pledged to provide affordable coverage for the more than 46 million Americans who had no health insurance. Finally, in March 2010, Congress passed the Affordable Care Act.

Less than two years into Obama's first term, the economy was still sluggish. Unemployment peaked at 10.2 percent in 2009. Although the economy had stabilized by the spring of 2010, unemployment remained high and growth was slow.

Some Americans, such as those in the Tea Party movement, felt that Obama's domestic programs were too costly and gave too much power to the federal government. Americans were also concerned about slow economic growth. In the 2010 elections, Republicans regained control of the House of Representatives.

The economy continued to remain a major concern for voters heading into the 2012 election. Obama's election campaign portrayed his opponent, Mitt Romney, as out of touch with ordinary people. This helped Obama win reelection.

TOPIC 13 LESSON 4

Lesson Summary
AMERICANS LOOK TO THE FUTURE

As the twenty-first century dawned, American society looked very different than it had a hundred years before. The Immigration Act of 1990 had increased quotas by 40 percent and eased most restrictions. Since then, almost one million immigrants arrived in the United States each year. Most of the new immigrants were Latinos. They have had a profound social, cultural, and political impact. Asian countries make up the second-largest source of the new immigration.

Some people worry that immigrants take jobs and social services away from native-born Americans. They oppose **bilingual education**, in which students are taught in their native languages as well as in English. Proponents of immigration argue that immigrants contribute to the economy and help the nation maintain its population. Much of the debate concerns illegal immigrants. The Immigration and Control Act of 1986 aimed to stop the flow of illegal immigrants by penalizing businesses that hired them, but illegal immigrants still regularly cross U.S. borders.

American demographics have changed, as many people have moved from the Midwest and the Northeast to the Sunbelt. The American family changed as well. Divorces and single-parent households are now more common than they were just 40 years ago.

Affirmative action was created in the 1960s to help minorities and women overcome past discrimination by giving them preference in school admissions and job applications. Today, such programs are being challenged and in some cases, ended. Even so, women and African Americans continue to make social and political gains. More African Americans now earn middle-class incomes and hold college degrees. Women are protected against unfair treatment in the workplace. The 1994 Violence Against Women Act increased federal resources to apprehend and prosecute men guilty of violent acts against women.

As the baby boom generation reaches retirement, falling birthrates mean there may not be enough workers to pay for their Social Security benefits. President Bush proposed **privatizing** Social Security. This change would allow younger workers to invest some of their earnings in individual retirement accounts. Opponents defeated his proposal and the debate continues.

Lesson Vocabulary

bilingual education   system in which students are taught in their native languages as well as in English

affirmative action   policy that gives special consideration to women and minorities to make up for past discrimination

privatizing   to transfer from governmental ownership or control to private interests

TOPIC 13 Review Questions

AMERICA IN THE TWENTY-FIRST CENTURY

Answer the questions below using the information in the Lesson Summaries on the previous pages.

Lesson 1: America and the World Economy

1. **Identify Main Ideas** What role did the United States play in global economics during the 1990s?

_____

_____

2. How did the rise of the service economy in the United States affect labor unions?

_____

_____

Lesson 2: The George W. Bush Presidency

3. Why was the outcome of the 2000 presidential election unusual?

_____

_____

4. **Recognize Sequence** Which event in Bush's presidency had the greatest influence on subsequent events? Explain.

_____

_____

_____

Lesson 3: The Barack Obama Presidency

5. What was the main issue voters were concerned about in 2008?

_____

_____

6. **Recognize Effects** What effect did slow economic growth have on the 2010 election?

_____

_____

Lesson 4: Americans Look to the Future

7. How have American demographics changed in recent decades?

_____

_____

8. **Identify Supporting Details** What law increased resources to prosecute men guilty of violence against women?

_____

_____